toys to sew

toys to sew

Claire Garland

COLLINS & BROWN

First published in the United Kingdom in 2006
First published in paperback in 2008 by
Collins & Brown
10 Southcombe Street
London
W14 0RA

An imprint of Anova Books Company Ltd

ISBN: 978-1-84340-469-9

A CIP catalogue record for this book is available from
the British Library.

10 9 8 7 6 5 4 3 2 1

Reproduction by Anorax
Printed and bound by SNP Leefung, China

Photography by Mark Winwood.

Keep updated. Email crafts@anovabooks.com

This book can be ordered direct from the publisher.
Contact the marketing department, but try your
bookshop first.

www.anovabooks.com

Contents

Introduction

The simplest toys are often the embodiment of happy childhood playtimes. Costumed rag dolls make the best guests at an afternoon tea party, while an easy-going stuffed animal in tow can be a loyal best friend at the playground. And embracing a favourite teddy makes for the safest and most comforting experience during naptime.

As a child, I was surrounded by toys. From a rag doll with missing stuffing to a bear whose fur had been worn away, my dearest companions may not have been in the most pristine condition, but they provided me with hours upon hours of amusement and I loved them all the same. Though I grew older and my interests broadened, I soon discovered that creating my very own toys was as much as fun as playing with them.

With *Toys to Sew*, I've designed a collection of dolls for children and adults alike by drawing inspiration from the dolls and stuffed animals of my childhood. Whether the doll is patched up or the animal boasts an odd-buttoned eye, each toy has its own personality and plenty of character to become a cherished lifelong pal. Everyone can enjoy working fabric into toys that will be adored forever.

This whimsical collection features dolls and toys that will appeal to children of all ages. She'll find plenty of entertainment playing dress up with the dolls and wardrobes from the first chapter. You'll also find a delightful assortment of toys in the Animals & Nursery Toys chapter. A floppy-eared pink elephant and an old-fashioned teddy bear make endearing playtime pals. And for your wee cowboy? The wild, wild West wouldn't be quite the same without a patchwork hobby horse. Furthermore, if you're new to the sewing process, simple projects such as the Bears in Waistcoats and the Retro Tea Set are ideal for beginners.

I loved playing with toys when I was child and I love sewing them for my children as an adult. Many of these toys are designed to entertain and amuse your children for years to come. It's always meant a great deal to have sewn something myself and I hope the toys you create from this book provide you and the children in your life with as much enjoyment as they have for me and my little ones.

Before You Begin

Basic kit

For each of the projects you will need a basic kit. Each toy has a pattern template (pages 70-95) and to use these, you will need a pencil, paper, carbon paper and a water-soluble fabric marker or air-erasable fabric marker. You will also need a needle (or sewing machine) and thread in appropriate colours for sewing the toys and garments. The basic kit is not listed in each individual project.

How to enlarge patterns and designs

Turn to pages 70–95 for the pattern templates for each project. Most pieces are printed as a scaled-down version in order to fit the page. To enlarge them to the correct size, simply photocopy the pattern using the enlargement button on the photocopier. Enlarge to 200% unless specified otherwise in the project. Place the templates on the wrong side of the fabric and draw around them.

Transferring patterns and markings to fabric

For heavy fabrics and coloured or patterned cottons, place carbon paper between the pattern and the wrong side of the fabric. Trace over it with a pencil or tracing wheel. Alternatively, cut out the pattern pieces and draw around them with a water-soluble fabric marker. Then mark the dots and other features with the carbon paper. Employ this method for transferring shapes for patchwork piecing.

For lightweight fabrics, trace the design using a water-soluble fabric marker. Tape the pattern piece to a window (in daylight) or a light-box. Place the fabric over it, right side up, and trace the lines on to the fabric.

To transfer dots, darts and other placement markings to fabric, pin the pattern to the wrong side of the fabric and insert a pin at the marking. Lift up the edge of the pattern and mark the fabric with a water-soluble fabric marker.

Symbols

Small triangles indicate where you should clip notches into the seam allowance. Notches prevent a seam from pulling and making the fabric pucker.

Positional dots are to assist with matching pieces together.

Sewing

The seam allowance is 6 mm (1/4 in), unless stated otherwise. All seams should be pinned and tacked before machine sewing or stitching by hand.

Sewing Skills

The next few pages provide information on the techniques you will need to complete the toys. The methods are easy to grasp; however, if you are new to sewing, it is advisable to start off creating simpler toys such as the Cat & Mouse Skittles.

Sewing techniques

Darts
A dart or a tapering tuck is added into the fabric to give shape to the finished article. It is marked as a large triangle with broken lines on the pattern, which is then transferred onto the fabric. With right sides together, fold the fabric along the centre of the dart matching the tapering stitch (broken) lines. Beginning at the widest part of the dart stitch up to the point. On fine fabrics, press the dart to one side. To reduce bulk on heavy fabrics such as felt, slash along the fold of the dart for about half its length, then press open with your finger.

Gathering
To gather fabric using a sewing machine, make a few parallel rows of long straight stitches, secured at one end. Pull the other end to gather, then secure it to hold the gathers.

To gather fabric by hand, make one or two rows of small running stitches, about 3–6 mm (⅛–¼ in) long, by knotting one end of the thread and pulling the other end to gather.

Clipping seam allowance
Curved seams should be clipped so that they will lie flat. After sewing, clip the seam allowance on both pieces of fabric to about 3 mm (⅛ in) from the stitching. Clip about every 2.5 cm (1 in), depending on the tightness of the curve. Tight curves will need clipping more frequently. Outer curves should be notched – clip a triangle out of the seam allowance. Clipped seams should be pressed open or pressed to one side.

Hemming corners
To reduce bulk at the corners of a hem, press the hem, then open it out at the corner and cut diagonally across the corner 3 mm (⅛ in) from the

allowance. Turn the diagonal edge under to the wrong side. Refold the hem. The diagonally folded edges should meet edge to edge forming a neat 45° angle at the hem edge. Slipstitch the mitred edges together, then stitch close to the inner edges of the hem.

Hand-sewing

Backstitch
Use for sewing strong seams or for attaching trims by hand. Bring the needle up from the underside of the fabric and insert it about 3 mm (⅛ in) behind the point at which the thread came out. Bring the needle out about 3 mm (⅛ in) in front of the starting point. Continue in the same manner.

Whipstitch
Use to attach a trim or join appliqué to the main fabric. Working from right to left, bring the needle out from the

back and through to the front. Re-insert the needle, making a diagonal stitch from the front to the back close to the edge of the fabric/trim to be joined. Repeat along the length making the stitches close together.

Tacking
Make long running stitches, about 6 mm (¼ in) or longer. (To tack by machine, use a straight stitch at the longest length possible.) To hold fabrics, trims and ribbons in place, make several small, straight stitches in the same spot.

Overcast stitch
Make diagonal stitches over the edge of the fabric to finish the edges.

Running stitch
Weave the needle in and out of the fabric, keeping the stitches small and even. Use for sewing seams by hand, tacking, gathering and quilting.

Slipstitch
Use to join two folded edges of fabric (for example at the mitred edge of a hem), secure bindings, or to close openings in seams. The stitches should be almost invisible. Working from right to left, bring the needle out through one folded edge. Pick up a few threads of the adjoining fabric and then a few threads on the folded edge. Repeat along the length.

Embroidery stitches

Chainstitch
Bring the needle up from the underside of the fabric at one end of the line to be embroidered. Loop the thread, then insert the needle next to where the thread came out. Bring it up again over the end of the looped thread. This forms a flat loop against the fabric. Repeat, keeping stitches the same length.

French knot
Bring the needle out on the surface of the fabric at the place where the knot is to lie. Wrap the thread around the needle two or three times, depending on how big you want the knot to be. Insert the needle close to where it came out. Holding the knot in place, pull the needle to the wrong side to secure the knot.

Satin stitch
Work parallel straight stitches, close together, across the entire area of a shape to fill it.

Stem stitch
Bring the needle to the front at the left-hand side of the working line. With the thread beneath the needle, take it through to the back just beneath the working line. Pull the needle through. The thread at this point creates a very slight diagonal to the working line.

Continue making these diagonal stitches along the working line, keeping all the stitches the same size.

Straight stitch
This stitch is used as an occasional single stitch scattered into a design, to form letters, or grouped into a ring to form a flower. Each stitch is always separated from the next one.

Dolls & Doll Clothes

Dolls can be the most endearing and characterful members of the toy chest. I've re-created some of my favourite dolls from my childhood, including *Sonny Sam* and *Binah Ballerina*, and designed various wardrobes to suit most occasions! From a daytime ensemble to outdoor gear, design a collection of fun and fashionable clothes that will keep your dolls looking their best all the time.

Basic Doll

The Basic Doll is the template for all the rag dolls in this book. I have made her in a simple calico but you could use an array of fabrics, including recycled materials from clothing or scraps left from other sewing projects.

Basic Doll

MATERIALS

- Calico (or fabric of your choice): 1 m (1 yd), 127 cm (50 in) wide
- White and pink felt scraps for mouth and colour of choice for eyes
- Black and pink embroidery thread for facial features
- Heavyweight yarn for hair
- Toy stuffing
- Embroidery needle (size 5 or 6)
- Large-eyed needle

Templates:
See page 72.

ARMS AND LEGS

1. With right sides together, stitch seams of the two arms, leaving shoulder seam open.

2. Turn right side out and stuff, using a pencil to make sure the stuffing is packed down firmly. Slipstitch the shoulder seams together to close.

3. To create the elbow joint, machine-stitch across the centre of each arm.

4. With right sides together, stitch the seams of the two legs, leaving top edges open.

5. Turn right side out and stuff as for the arms. Slipstitch the top edges together to close.

HEAD AND BODY

6. Using black embroidery thread, join the irises to the outer eyes by working a French knot in the centre. Sew in place on the face using the pattern piece as a positional guide, then work small stitches around the eyes (see photo). Use pink embroidery thread to sew on the mouth.

7. With right sides together, sew the front of the body and head to the back of the body and head, leaving the straight edge at the base of the body open. Leave two spaces between the notches on the shoulders for inserting the arms. Clip the seam allowance at the neck.

8. Turn right side out and press lightly. Press the seam allowance at the openings under. Pin the arms in position and hand-stitch firmly in place.

9. Stuff the body and head firmly through the opening, pin the legs in position, then hand-stitch in place, closing the opening at the base of the body.

HAIR

10. To create the hair, cut lengths of yarn to double the desired finished length.

11. To sew on the hair, begin with a 'foundation piece' – take one length of yarn and lay it across the seam at the top of the head. Whipstitch along its length to join it to the head. (Further foundation pieces can be sewn on in lines across the back of the head from ear to ear; it depends

how much coverage you want.)

12. To attach each length of hair, fold the strand in half and thread the folded end through the large-eyed needle. Pass the needle through the foundation piece, remove the needle as it emerges and then pull the cut ends of the yarn through the loop and draw up to make a knot that lies against the foundation piece. Work further strands of hair along the foundation piece (and any subsequent foundation pieces across the back of the head) to complete. Trim if necessary.

Underwear

MATERIALS

- Cotton fabric: 30 x 10 cm (12 x 4 in)
- Elasticized lace edging: 50 cm (20 in)

Template:
See page 72.

MAKING UP

1. Fold in half, right sides together, and sew the side seams. Turn right side out.

2. At the leg openings, turn 6 mm (1/4 in) to the wrong side, then tack and sew the elasticized edging around the leg openings, pulling the elastic slightly so it will ruche when released.

3. At the waist edge, turn 6 mm (1/4 in) to the wrong side, tack and sew on edging, again pulling the elastic taut (a little more than for the legs) so it will ruche as before.

Camisole

MATERIALS

- Cotton fabric: 30 x 15 cm (12 x 6 in)
- Ricrac braid: 70 cm (28 in)
- Elasticized lace edging: 25 cm (10 in)

Template:
See page 73.

MAKING UP

1. With the right sides of the front and back together, sew the side seams. Sew the shoulder seams.

2. At the armholes, turn a 3 mm (1/8 in) hem to the wrong side. Stitch in place. Trim on the right side with ricrac braid.

3. At the waist edge, turn a double 6 mm (1/4 in) hem to the inside and stitch in place. Trim on the right side with more ricrac braid.

4. At the neck edge, turn a 3 mm (1/8 in) hem to the wrong side. Stitch in place. Tack and sew the elasticized edging to the right side, pulling the elastic slightly so it will ruche when released.

Simple Clothes

The following patterns are basic silhouettes which can be adjusted to create the clothing throughout the book. Or better yet, indulge your creativity by using your favourite fabrics and embellishments to design your own collections – the possibilities are limitless!

Simple Trousers

MATERIALS
- Cotton fabric: 25 x 48 cm (10 x 19 in)
- Elastic: 6 mm (1/4 in) wide, 22 cm (8¾ in) long

Template:
See page 73.

MAKING UP
1. With right sides together, stitch the two back pieces together along the centre lines, from dot to dot.
2. With right sides together, stitch the two front pieces along the centre lines, from dot to dot.
3. With right sides of front and back together, align the gusset seams and sew front to back. Repeat with side seams. Turn right side out. Clip the seam allowance between the legs.
4. Turn bottom edge under

6 mm (1/4 in) to create hem and hand-stitch in place with a neat running stitch.
5. At the waist, fold edge under 1.3 cm (1/2 in) twice to the wrong side to make a casing and fold the raw edge

under. Sew the casing in place 1 cm (3/8 in) from the upper edge. Leave 6 mm (1/4 in) opening in the line of stitching. Thread the elastic through the casing using a safety pin. Pull the elastic to the desired waist

width. Join the ends securely and let them slide inside the casing. Slipstitch the casing to close.

Sleeveless Top

MATERIALS
- Felt: 13 x 16 cm (5¼ x 6¼ in)
- Felt scraps for the motif
- Braid, trim or ribbon, 32 cm (12¾ in) for the edging

Templates:
See page 73.

MAKING UP
1. With right sides together, align and then sew the side seams and shoulder seams, joining back to front.
2. Hand stitch the trim/braid to the waist edge.
3. Cut out a simple motif and join with a stitch or two to the front of the top.

Basic Shoes/Boots

MATERIALS
- Felt: 12 cm (5 in) square for soles; 23 cm (9 in) square for uppers
- Felt, ribbon or braid scraps for decoration
- Yarn scraps for laces

SEWING SHOES
Template:
See page 73.

1. With the right sides together, stitch the back seam on each upper. Stitch the dart on each toe.
2. Turn right side out. Put under a cloth and gently press the seam and the dart flat.
3. With the wrong sides uppermost, match the dots on the upper with the sole. Join the two pieces with a running stitch or carefully machine in place. Trim the surplus fabric close to the stitching and turn right side out.
4. Attach a scrap of ribbon or braid across the shoe to make a strap and sew on a decorative motif if desired.

SEWING BOOTS
Templates:
See page 78.

1. Placing the right sides together, stitch the front to the back along the back seam. Stitch around the toe and along the upper, or halfway along the upper if you wish to add laces.
2. Turn right side out and use your fingers to smooth out the seams and make them lie flat.
3. With the wrong sides uppermost, match the dots on the upper with the sole. Join the two pieces with a running stitch or carefully machine in place. Trim the surplus fabric close to the stitching and turn right side out.
4. If desired, sew on laces using a large-eyed needle.

Day Clothes

Who said one has to sacrifice style for comfort? This adorable ensemble will have your fashion-minded doll looking spot on in a fur vest, a miniskirt with a pompom hem and striped socks. Create an outfit for every day of the week with leftover fabrics!

Mini Skirt

MATERIALS

- Cotton fabric: two x 22 cm (8¾ in) squares
- Elastic: 6 mm (¼ in) wide, 24 cm (9½ in) long
- Ribbon or trim: 46 cm (18 in)

Template:
See page 74.

MAKING UP

1. With right sides together, align and then sew the side seams, joining back to front. Stitch the darts and press the pleats. Turn right side out.
2. Turn under 2.5 cm (1 in) to make a hem and tack in place. Stitch the hem 2 cm (¾ in) from the lower edge.
3. At the waist, fold edge under 1.3 cm (½ in) twice to the wrong side to make a casing and fold the raw edge under. Sew the casing in place 1 cm (⅜ in) from the upper edge. Leave a 6 mm (¼ in) opening in the line of stitching. Thread the elastic through the casing using a safety pin. Pull the elastic to the desired waist width. Join the ends securely and slide them inside the casing. Slipstitch the opening in the casing to close.
4. Sew the trim or ribbon to the bottom of the skirt.

Fur Vest

MATERIALS

- Fleece fabric: 40 cm (16 in) square
- Fluffy trim: 1 m (1 yard)
- Bead or toggle

Templates:
See page 74.

MAKING UP

1. With right sides together, stitch the fronts to the back at the shoulder seam. Join the side seams. Stitch the pleat in the back neck edge.
2. With right sides facing, sew together the two hood pieces from head to centre back.
3. Ease the hood around the neck edge of the vest and sew in place. Trim the felt close to the seam. Stitch the trim in place around the hem and around the edge of the hood.
4. Sew the bead or toggle to one side of the vest; cut a slit in the opposite side of the vest to create a buttonhole.

Socks

MATERIALS

- Old pair of child's socks retaining the elasticized edges of the socks as the doll's sock tops.

Template:
See page 74.

MAKING UP

1. With right sides together, sew the seams for both socks. Turn right side out.

Outdoor Clothes

Here are some outdoor clothes that any doll would like to be seen in when she's out and about. The poncho, flared trousers and gloves are easy to make from scraps and fit all the dolls.

Poncho

MATERIALS
- Child's old cardigan or sweater
- Thin card cut into two x 5 cm (2 in) diameter circles for a pompom maker
- Twisted cord
- Scrap of felt for binding
- Tapestry yarn for tassels

Template:
See page 75.

MAKING UP
1. Make two pompoms from leftover wool. Cut a 2.5 cm (1 in) diameter hole in the centre of each card circle, then place the two circles together. Thread a large sewing needle with as many ends of yarn as it will take. The lengths should be about 1 m (1 yd). Hold the two circles of card together and thread the needle through the centre, around the outside and back through the centre from the front, continue to wind like this until the centre hole is full – you will need to hold the tail in place with your thumb when you first begin to wind. Using a sharp pair of scissors, cut around the pompom in between the two card discs. This done, card still in place, tie a length of yarn (about 20 cm [8 in]) around the centre of the pompom as tightly as possible and then remove the card

circles. Trim the pompom to fluff it a bit and form a ball.

2. Knot three 1 m (1 yd) lengths of yarn together at one end, then twist the lengths tightly together. Holding the free ends, fold the twist in half so that the free ends and the knotted ends meet. The yarn will twist itself together into a cord. Tie the free ends and knotted ends together and even out any bumps. Cut the cord in half and knot the cut ends. Sew the cords to the pompoms.

3. With right sides together, pin the side seams, at the same time adding a twisted cord at each end of neck edge.

4. Sew the seams, catching in the cords. Turn right side out.

5. Cut a 2.5 cm (1 in) x 30 cm (12 in) strip of felt and, folding it lengthways, ease it over the neck edge to bind the raw edges. Stitch in place overlapping where the ends meet. Trim if necessary.

6. Turn a 2.5 cm (1 in) hem to the wrong side and sew in place.

7. Cut the tapestry yarn into 10 cm (4 in) lengths. Fold each strand in half and thread the loop created into the needle eye. Thread the strand through the stitches at the bottom edge of the poncho, passing the needle through the looped end as the needle emerges. Pull to tighten and release the needle. Trim fringe.

Trousers

MATERIALS
- Sleeves of an old long-sleeved T-shirt
- For the trouser ties: 50 cm (16¾ in) length of embroidery silk
- Six beads for decoration

Follow instructions to create Simple Trousers (see page 17) and adjust to longer length. Instead of threading elastic through the waist casing, use embroidery silk, pulling both ends out at the gap. Turn the ends at opening and stitch in place to conceal the raw edges. To secure the silk, thread three beads onto the ends of the ties before knotting the ends.

Gloves

MATERIALS
- A baby's old cardigan
- Fancy elasticized trim: 10 cm (4 in)

Template:
See page 75.

MAKING UP
1. With right sides together, carefully sew around the sides and thumb seam with a 3 mm (⅛ in) seam allowance. Turn right side out.

2. Turn a 1 cm (⅜ in) hem to the wrong side at the cuff edge and stitch in place. Sew on the elasticized trim around the cuff edge.

Nightclothes

Putting dolly to bed can be a good way of introducing the unpopular notion of bedtime to a child. These nightclothes fit all the dolls. You could also make the '50s shirt on page 28 as a pyjama top.

Pyjama Top

MATERIALS
- Cotton or flannel:
  one piece, 20 x 30 cm
  (8 x 12 in) for bodice; one
  piece, 10 x 25 cm (4 x 10 in)
  for skirt; one piece, 25 x 40
  cm (10 x 16 in) for trousers
- Bias binding: 6 mm x 22 cm
  (¼ x 8¾ in)
- Elastic: 6 mm (¼ in) wide,
  22 cm (8¼ in) long

Templates:
See page 76.

MAKING UP
1. Press 6 mm (¼ in) to wrong
side on centre back edges.
2. Stitch along the edge 4 mm
(⅕ in) from the fold line.
3. With the right sides of the
fronts and backs together, sew
the side seams. Sew the
shoulder seams.
4. At the armholes, turn a
3 mm (⅛ in) hem to the wrong

side. Stitch in place.

5. Fold the bias binding over the neck edge and sew it in place.

6. Overlap the centre back edges to seam allowance and join 2.5 cm (1 in) from waist edge.

7. To make the skirt, fold the fabric in half lengthways with right sides together and gently press the fold. Sew back seam. Turn right side out.

8. At the raw waist edge, run a row of gathering stitches. Pull up to fit the circumference of the bodice.

9. Pin raw edge of top and skirt together, then stitch together with a 2 cm (¾ in) seam allowance.

Pyjama Trousers

As Simple Trousers adjusted to mid length (see page 17).

Robe

MATERIALS
- Terry cloth: 50 cm (20 in), 112 cm (45 in) wide
- Cotton or flannel: one strip, 8 x 84 cm (3¼ x 33 in) (belt)

Template:
See pages 75-76.

MAKING UP
1. With right sides together, stitch the fronts to the back at the shoulder. Turn right side out.
2. Fold the front facings to the wrong side and stitch along the inner edge of facings.
3. With the right sides together, ease the sleeves to fit the armhole edges and stitch the seams.
4. Turn under 12 mm (½ in) hems at each sleeve edge.
5. Still with right sides together, stitch the back to the fronts along the side seams and underarms.
6. Join the hood along the top and centre back seam. Fold under a 12 mm (½ in) hem around the front edge of hood and stitch in place.
7. Ease the hood along the neck edge of the gown, aligning dots, and stitch the seam.
8. Hem the lower edge of the robe.
9. Hem along one edge of the pocket. Turn under 6mm (¼ in) on other three sides. Pin then tack into position onto one front. Stitch in place along all three unhemmed seams. Remove the tacking stitches.
10. With two 12 cm (4¾ in) strands of embroidery silk or fine cord make belt loops by threading each end, 2.5 cm (1 in) apart, through the side seam then securing on the wrong side of the robe with a couple of stitches.
11. With right sides together, fold the belt in half along the length. Sew along one short edge and the long edge.
12. Turn right side out through the open end. Press.
13. Turn in the raw edges at the open end then whipstitch the opening to close. Thread through the loops.

Bunny Slippers

MATERIALS
- Red fleece: 12 cm (5 in) square for soles; 23 cm (9 in) square for uppers
- Two black beads for eyes
- White felt scrap for ears

Template:
See page 76.

As Basic Shoes (see page 18). Sew two eyes and two ears to each slipper for the bunny's face.

Sonny Sam

This cheeky chap is likely to become a firm favourite. He's dressed in a striking raincoat, gingham shorts, beanie and baseball boots.

MATERIALS

Doll
- Natural colour linen: 1 m (1 yd) square
- White, blue/brown and pink felt scraps for eyes and mouth
- Black and pink embroidery thread for facial features
- Orange heavyweight yarn for hair
- Toy stuffing
- Embroidery needle (size 5 or 6)

Raincoat
- Red PVC: 50 cm (20 in), 112 cm (45 in) wide
- Two blue buttons

Shorts
- Patterned cotton fabric: 50 cm (20 in) square
- Elastic: 6 mm (¼ in) wide, 22 cm (8¼ in) long

Baseball boots
- Felt: 12 cm (5 in) square, cream for soles; 23 cm (9 in) square denim blue for uppers; cream scrap for tongue
- Two pieces of heavyweight yarn for bootlaces
- Bradawl or very large-eyed needle

Beanie hat
- Jersey fabric: two x 15 cm (6 in) squares

Template:
See pages 77-78.

Doll and Hair

As for Basic Doll (see page 14).

Baseball Boots

MAKING UP
1. With right sides together, stitch the back seam on each upper. Turn right side out and gently press the seam flat under a cloth. Using a zigzag stitch, stitch a line that traces the heel area of the boot.
2. With right sides together, stitch the toe seam on each upper. Press the seam flat. Turn right side out.
3. With a bradawl or very large-eyed needle, make six eyelet holes for the laces along either side of the boot.
4. Hand-sew the tongue behind the front opening. Thread the laces through the eyelet holes.
5. Matching front and back notches to the side seams, sew the sole to the uppers using blanket stitch.

Shorts

As Simple Trousers (see page 17). Use pattern at the short length, sew up as trousers, turning up the hemmed edges by 6 mm (¼ in).

Shirt

MATERIALS

- Patterned cotton fabric: 50 cm (20 in) square
- Two 15 cm (6 in) cotton ties

Templates:
See page 77.

MAKING UP

1. With right sides together, stitch the collar pieces together along the two straight edges. Clip the corners and then turn right side out. Turn under the raw edges to the wrong side and press.

2. With right sides together, stitch the shirt fronts to the shirt back at shoulder seams.

3. Tack the collar to the right side of the neck edge, matching the dots on the fronts with the dots on the collar. Stitch in place. Remove the tacking stitches.

4. Press 12 mm (½ in) to the wrong side on the centre front edges. Turn under the raw edges.

5. Stitch along the inner edge of the facings and 6 mm (¼ in) from the fold line.

6. With the right sides together, ease the sleeves to fit the armhole edges and stitch the seams.

7. Turn under a 6 mm (¼ in) hem at each sleeve edge.

8. With right sides together, stitch the shirt back to the shirt fronts along the side seams and underarms.

9. Hem the lower edge of the shirt with a double 6 mm (¼ in) allowance.

10. Attach the ties at the collar/neck edge.

Chunky Sweater

MATERIALS

- An old sweater
- Felt scraps for motif

Templates:
See page 77.

MAKING UP

1. Draw, transfer, then cut out a motif from the felt scrap.

2. Hand-stitch the motif to the sweater front.

3. With right sides together, stitch the sweater front to the

back at the shoulder seams.

4. Ease the sleeves to fit the armhole edges and stitch seams.

5. Stitch together the sleeve seams and side seams.

6. Cut neck from a ribbed edge of old sweater if you can and stitch the seam if necessary. Roll down.

7. With right sides facing, ease the polo neck around the neck edge and sew in place. Turn out the right way.

8. If you have managed to retain the original waist and sleeve edges, it is not necessary to hem. Otherwise, sew a 2.5 cm (1 in) hem on the waist and sleeves.

Raincoat

MAKING UP

1. With right sides together, stitch the fronts to the back at the shoulder seams.

2. With right sides together, ease the sleeves into the armholes, then stitch.

3. With right sides together, stitch the fronts to the back along the side and underarm seams. Turn right side out.

4. Sew the top seam of the hood and with right sides together, ease it to fit the neck edge between the notches.

5. Measure the diameter of the buttons, add on the depth of the button plus 2 mm ($^1/_{16}$ in). Evenly spaced down one front edge, cut two horizontal slits

to this measurement for the buttonholes. Sew on the buttons to match the holes.

Beanie Hat

MAKING UP

1. With right sides together, stitch along the round edge, leaving the straight edge open.

2. Turn right side out.

3. Fold under a 2.5 cm (1 in) hem on the straight edge, then fold again to conceal raw edge. Stitch in place with a double line of stitching.

Binah Ballerina

Dressed in a rose-sprinkled tutu and ballet slippers, this winsome doll is set for the gala performance of the season! She will undoubtedly win the heart of any little girl, sitting pretty by the windowsill or pirouetting across a room.

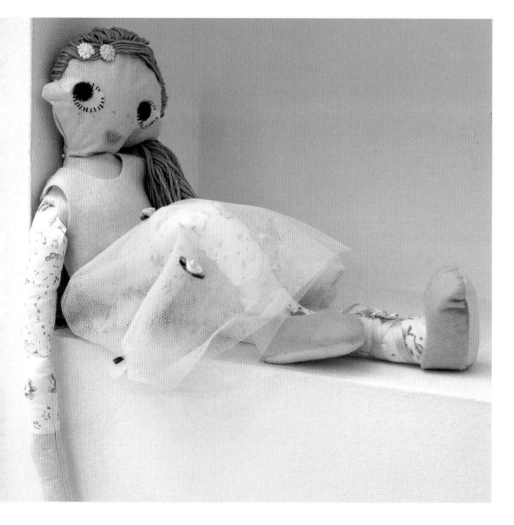

MATERIALS

Doll

- Calico: 50 cm (20 in), 127 cm (50 in) wide for body/head, hands, underwear
- Patterned cotton: 25 x 20 cm (10 x 8in) for arms and legs
- Black, brown and pink embroidery thread for face
- Gold chenille yarn for hair
- Two buttons for hairslide
- Decorative elastic: 30 cm (12 in) for stockings
- Toy stuffing
- Embroidery needle (size 5 or 6)

Tutu

- Net: two x 40 x 50 cm (16 x 20 in) for skirt
- Elastic: 6 mm (¼ in) wide, 20 cm (8 in) long
- Felt: two x 15 cm (6 in) squares, cream for bodice
- Decorative ribbon or braid: 70 cm (28 in) for sash
- Six ribbon roses in pink and cream

- Velvet or satin ribbon: two pieces, 2.5 cm (1 in) wide, 15 cm (6 in) long for bodice straps, plus extra for bow in hair

Dance slippers
- Felt: 12 cm (5 in) square, cream for soles; 16 cm (6¼ in) square, pale pink for uppers
- Narrow satin ribbon: 6 mm (¼ in) wide, two x pieces 50 cm (20 in) long for ties

Templates:
See page 79.

Doll

As for Basic Doll (see page 14), using patterned fabric for arms and calico for hands. Scatter a few freckles on her face by working French knots.

Hair

As Basic Doll. Carry some strands across the hairline to make a fringe and secure with two buttons to make hairslide. Tie hair in ribbon.

Stockings

As legs for Basic Doll using patterned fabric.

Tutu

MAKING UP
1. Fold each piece of net in half lengthways and gently press the fold with a cool iron. With right sides of both pieces together, sew the back seam through all four layers of net.
2. At the raw waist edge, turn the 2.5 cm (1 in) allowance for the casing to the wrong side and then fold the raw edge under. Sew casing in place 1 cm (3/8 in) from the upper edge. Leave a 6 mm (¼ in) opening in the line of stitching for inserting elastic. Thread elastic through casing using a safety pin. Pull elastic to desired waist width. Join ends securely and slide them inside the casing. Slipstitch casing to close.
3. With right sides together, stitch front bodice to back at side seams. Sew the ribbon straps at each shoulder, with the right side of the ribbon facing the right side of the bodice front. Cross the straps and catch to the inside of the back bodice.
4. Join the bodice to the skirt by tucking the top of the skirt inside the bodice. Stitch along the bottom of the bodice or whipstitch the bodice to the skirt. Sew the decorative ribbon around the waist to make sash and tie into a bow. Randomly sew on roses.

Dance Slippers

MAKING UP
1. With right sides together, stitch back seam on each upper.
2. Turn right side out and gently press seam flat.
3. Work a gathering stitch along the toe seams of each upper and gather up to fit around the toe end of each sole.
4. Matching the dots on the uppers with the soles, join upper and sole with right sides together and use a running stitch or machine stitch to sew the seam.
5. Fold each ribbon tie in half and sew fold into back seam.

Jolly Pirate Pal

Ahoy, matey! This dramatic character has led an adventurous life on the high seas. His outfit can easily be further adapted to make an array of clothes for other brave and popular heroes.

MATERIALS

Doll
- Natural colour linen or pure cotton sheeting: 1 m (1 yd) square
- Striped fabric: 30 x 40 cm (12 x 16 in) for legs
- White, blue/brown and pink felt scraps for eyes and mouth
- Black and pink embroidery thread for facial features
- Narrow gold braid for earrings
- Toy stuffing
- Embroidery needle (size 5 or 6)

Shirt
- White cotton fabric: 50 cm (20 in) square

Vest
- Black felt: 30 cm (12 in) square

Trousers
- Denim blue felt: 50 cm (20 in) square

- Braid: 35 cm (14 in) for waistband

Boots
- Black felt: 12 cm (5 in) square for soles; 23 cm (9 in) square uppers
- 2 pieces of 2-ply yarn for bootlaces

Bandana
- Child's polka dot sock

Templates:
See page 79.

Doll

As for Basic Doll (see page 14). Use linen. Stitch on facial stubble by working a scattering of straight stitches. Attach a loop of gold braid to each ear for earrings.

Shirt

MAKING UP
1. Make the Mini Skirt (see page 20) at the short length, leaving a gap in each side seam near the top to form the armholes.
2. Fold under 6 mm (¼ in) hem twice at each armhole edge.
3. Hand-stitch a vertical row of gathering stitches at the centre of the lower part of each sleeve and pull up to produce a ruched effect. Secure ends.
4. Gather top edge of each sleeve. With right sides together, stitch sleeve seam.
5. Turn up the hem of the sleeve and stitch in place. Turn right side out.
6. With right sides together, ease the sleeves into the armholes and stitch the seams.

Vest

MAKING UP

1. With right sides together, stitch the fronts to the back at the shoulder and side seams.
2. Stitch the dart in the back.
3. Flatten the seams with your fingers and turn the vest right side out.

Trousers

MAKING UP

1. With right sides together, make as for the Simple Trousers at mid length (see page 17), adding the darts as the pattern instructs.
2. Attach a length of braid at the back of the trousers. When the pirate is dressed, wind the braid twice around his waist and tie it firmly to keep his trousers up.

Boots

As Basic Boots (see page 18).

Bandana

Pull the open end of the sock on the pirate's head and knot the bandana behind his head.

Fairy Angel

Shiny, sparkly and magical, this blue-eyed treasure comes with a simple white dress, feathered wings and dazzling slippers. With a wand in hand, she's sure to cast a spell on your little angel. The doll requires little investment in time as well, so it makes an ideal gift for any youngster.

MATERIALS

Doll

- Linen or pure cotton sheeting: 1 m (1 yd) square
- White, blue or brown, and pink felt scraps for eyes and mouth
- Black and pink embroidery thread for facial features
- Chunky cream yarn for hair
- Shiny beads for tiara
- Toy stuffing
- Embroidery needle (size 5 or 6)

Dress and wings

- White cotton sheeting: 50 cm (20 in) square for dress; two x 20 x 2.5 cm (8 x 1 in) strips for sleeves
- Fluffy trim: 50 cm (20 in) for wings
- Elastic: 6 mm (¼ in) wide, 50 cm (20 in) long for neck and sleeves
- Sequins and beads

Slippers

- Cream felt: 12 cm (5 in) square for soles; 23 cm (9 in) square for uppers
- Sequins
- Sparkly ribbon: 25 cm (10 in) for ties

Wand

- Gold felt: 10 cm (4 in) square, plus a scrap for star
- Sequins

Templates:
See page 79.

Doll and Hair

As for Basic Doll (see page 14). Sew on sparkly beads at the hairline as a tiara.

Slippers

As Dance Slippers (see page 31). Embellish with sequins and ribbons, referring to the photograph.

Dress and Wings

MAKING UP

1. Make dress as for Mini Skirt (see page 20). Use pattern at long length. With right sides together, sew the dress, leaving two gaps in the side seams to insert the sleeves. Turn right side out and press the seams at armholes to the inside to conceal raw edges.

2. Make the puffed sleeves by folding each strip in half lengthways, with right sides together. Stitch along long edge. Turn right side out. Insert a 15 cm (6 in) length of elastic inside fabric tube and knot or sew ends of elastic together to create a 'scrunchie' or puff sleeve. Whipstitch short ends of fabric together. Sew the sleeve into the armhole opening.

3. Place the sleeve in the armhole and whipstitch to the dress. Make the other sleeve in the same way.

4. Decorate the dress with sequins and beads.

5. Twist the fluffy trim into a figure of eight twice, making two of the loops larger than the other two. Sew over the twist to secure, then stitch to the shoulder blades of the dress to secure.

Wand

MAKING UP

1. Roll up the square of felt and whipstitch along the join. Sew the star to the top of the wand and add a sequin. Sew to hand.

Animals & Nursery Toys

Stuffed animals always garner smiles and love from tots. From a friendly tortoise and a cheeky monkey to a button-eyed croc and a pink elephant, each member of this kingdom makes a worthy friend for your child. Pull-Along Nellie is patchwork perfection and Smart Bear makes a classic heirloom treasure. I've also included traditional nursery toys updated with new fabrics and inspired by retro styles.

Pink Elephant

Soft, downy fleece makes this pint-sized pachyderm a huggable favourite with little ones. This 'cuddle me' creature boasts bright floppy gingham ears and sewn on tusks; while his fleece scarf keeps him looking dapper when he's up to mischief.

MATERIALS

- Pink fleece: 50 cm (20 in), 112 cm (45 in) wide
- Cotton gingham fabric: two x 20 cm (8 in) squares for inner ears
- Buttons: two x 2 cm (¾ in) in diameter
- Ivory felt scraps for tusks
- Mixed felt scraps: eight pieces of 10 x 6 cm (4 x 2½ in) for patchwork upper scarf; one piece 80 x 6 cm (32 x 2½ in) for underside of scarf
- Toy stuffing

Templates:
See pages 80-81.

ELEPHANT
1. With right sides together, sew inner ear to outer ear, leaving top straight edge open. Turn right side out.
2. With right sides together, join the two trunk pieces, leaving the top edge open.

3. With right sides together, join the nose end of the head top to the top edge of the trunk.

4. Pin the ears at either side of the head top, matching notches and with the outer ear facing the right side of the fleece. Tack in place.

5. With right sides together, pin the head top to the head sides, matching notches and catching in the ears at the seams. Sew in place.

6. With right sides together, sew the seam that runs under the chin and along the trunk. Clip the seam allowance at the trunk end. Turn right side out.

LEGS

7. With right sides together, sew body back/outer front legs to the inner front legs, leaving the straight edge at the top of the leg open. Clip the seam allowance. Turn right side out.

8. With right sides together, join the body back/outer hind legs along the front and back seams. With right sides together, ease in the feet at the bottom of the leg pads and stitch in place. Leave the

straight edge at the top of the leg open. Turn right side out.

BODY BACK

9. With right sides together, fold the tail in half lengthways and stitch along the long edge. Turn right side out and fringe the tail end.

10. Join the two pieces for the body back/outer legs, catching in the tail, by placing them with right sides together with the tail sandwiched in between. Stitch to just past the tail on the body back and clip seam at this point. Turn right side out. With wrong sides together, stitch the remainder of the seam along the body back. Trim seam to 3 mm (½ in).

11. Stitch the body back to the head, beginning and ending under the chin.

BODY FRONT

12. Stitch the dart on the wrong side. With right sides together, sew the body front to the body back and inner legs, leaving a gap for stuffing.

STUFFING

13. Turn the whole elephant the right way out through the gap. Stuff, using a pencil to pack the stuffing into the trunk and legs.

14. Hand-sew the buttons for eyes and felt tusks in position.

SCARF

15. Join the eight rectangles as you would a strip of patchwork. With right sides together, place the upper scarf on the underside of the scarf and sew along the long edges and one short edge. Turn out through the other short end. Press to flatten.

16. Turn the seam allowance at the short end to the wrong side and hand-stitch to close.

Button-Eyed Crocodile

Even this cheerful chap loves a little game of hide and seek. Panels of terry cloth, fleece and cotton waffle sewn together create his wonderfully textured and multi-hued skin. With a playful spirit and a zig-zag stitched smile, this patchwork perfection certainly leaves us green with envy.

MATERIALS

- Cotton or terry cloth fabric: 14 x 15 cm (6 in) squares for body and legs
- White cotton fabric: 20 cm (8 in) square for eyes
- Two buttons
- White yarn for eyes and teeth
- Toy stuffing

Templates:
See page 82.

PATCHWORK SQUARES

1. Plan the placement of the fabric pieces, seven squares long by two squares wide, and mark the order in which they are placed by numbering them in pencil on the wrong side.
2. To join the squares, place right sides together and sew along each adjacent edge. Press the seams open.
3. Put the pattern pieces on the wrong side of the patchwork and transfer shapes.

LEGS AND BODY

4. With right sides together, join the pieces for each leg, leaving the straight edge at the top open. Turn right side out and stuff lightly.
5. With right sides together, join one body piece to the other, at the same time placing the raw edges of the legs at the seam along the underside of the body (leave a gap in the underside for stuffing). Turn the body the right way out through the gap. Stuff firmly and stitch the gap to close (the legs hang from the belly in pairs).

EYES

6. With right sides together, stitch around each eye shape, leaving the straight edge open. Turn right side out.
7. Sew a button to each eye with white yarn. On straight edge of eye, press a 6 mm (¼ in) hem to the wrong side.
Stuff each eye, then whipstitch it to the top of the head (see photo).
8. Cut a length of white yarn. approx. 25 cm (10 in) long, for the teeth. Secure one end of the yarn below and in front of the eye. Map out the zigzag of teeth around the head, pinning the yarn in position and tacking it in place.
9. Thread a needle with another 25 cm (10 in) of white yarn. Secure the yarn in the same place where you began the zigzag.
10. Following the line of the zigzag, fix each point with a small vertical stitch.
11. At the end of the zigzag, secure both threads.

Sock Cuddlies

Comprised of a cool-hand tiger, his easy-going doggy best mate, a flirty monkey and a spotted dalmatian, these super-cute cuddlies are a fabulous way of using up odd socks. Felted details give plenty of personality to this friendly gang of four.

Note:
See page 84-85 for all sock cuddly templates. Position all pattern pieces on socks as directed on templates.

Dog

MATERIALS
- Three odd adult's socks (or one pair and one odd) for body, head, arm, legs, ears
- Black felt scraps for eyes and nose; brown for patch
- One child's sock for sleeveless sweater
- Ricrac braid: 12 cm (4¾ in) to decorate top of legs
- Embroidery silk for facial features
- Two black beads
- Toy stuffing

ARMS AND LEGS
1. With right sides together, fold each arm in half lengthways and stitch the side seam, leaving the shoulder seam open.

2. Turn right side out and stuff, using a pencil to make sure the stuffing is packed down firmly. Sew across the shoulder seam.
3. Make the legs in the same way as the arms.

BODY
4. Use the leg part of a ribbed sock for the body.
5. Turn under the seam allowance along the openings.
6. Pin the legs at the bottom seam and hand-stitch firmly in place through all layers. Hand-stitch the remaining gap at the bottom seam to close.
7. Stuff the body firmly through the neck opening. Pin the arms at the neck seam and hand-stitch firmly in place through all layers. Hand-stitch the remaining gap to close.
8. Sew ricrac braid where the legs join the body.

HEAD
9. The head of the dog is made from the heel of one sock: the back of the head being the heel, the chin being the folded upper edge of the foot of the sock. With the heel/foot of the sock right sides together, stitch the muzzle seam. Turn right side out through the neck.
10. Sew felt patch, nose and eyes in place. Use embroidery silk for the facial features. Sew on two beads for centres of the eyes.
11. With right sides together, sew the seams of the ear pieces, leaving the top straight edge open. Turn right side out and stuff lightly. Fold the seam allowance to the inside.
12. Sew ears to the head.
13. Stuff the head firmly and sew to the body at neck edge.

SLEEVELESS SWEATER
14. Use the leg of the child's sock, with the elasticized top

as the neck of the sweater. If required, turn in a 2 cm (¾ in) hem at the bottom of the sweater and sew. For armholes, make cuts (the width of the arms) in the sides of the sweater, 2 cm (¾ in) down from the elasticized edge. Bind the edges by machine zigzag or whipstitch by hand.

Tiger

MATERIALS

- Three adult's socks for body, head, arm, legs, ears
- Felt scraps in assorted colours for facial features and motif
- Yellow felt: 20 cm (8 in) square for trousers
- Black heavyweight yarn for fur stripes
- Embroidery silk of your choice for facial features and whiskers
- Two black beads
- Two white sequins
- Ricrac braid: 50 cm (20 in) to decorate hem of trousers
- Toy stuffing

MAKING UP

1. Make arms, legs, body and head as for Dog.

2. Stitch nose and mouth in place. Stitch on sequins and beads for eyes. Embroider stripes on head.

3. For the whiskers, fold a strand of taupe sewing thread in half and pass the looped end through the eye of a needle. Push the needle through the fabric in the position of a whisker, remove the needle and pull the ends of the thread through the loop. Pull up so the loop lies against the nose.

TROUSERS

4. The seam allowance on the trousers is 3 mm (⅛ in). With right sides together, fold each trouser leg in half and stitch the leg seam.

5. With right sides together, stitch the crotch seam.

6. Clip into the seam allowance between the legs.

7. Use sock top for waistband and stitch to the waist edge of the trousers.

8. Stitch the motif on the front

of the trousers and trim the hems with ricrac braid.

Monkey

MATERIALS

- Three odd adult's socks (or one odd and a pair) for body, head, arm, legs, ears
- White felt scraps for face; pink for flower motif
- Blue felt: 20 cm (8 in) square for dress
- Black and beige embroidery silk for facial features
- Ricrac braid: 90 cm (36 in)
- Toy stuffing

MAKING UP

1. Place two arm pieces together, right sides facing and join leaving short, straight edge open.

2. Turn out and stuff, using a pencil to make sure the stuffing is packed down firmly. Hand stitch across the shoulder seam. Make the other arm in the same way.

3. To make the legs, follow the directions for making the arms.

4. With right sides together, join the two body pieces,

leaving the neck and bottom seam unstitched.

5. With the right sides of the sock facing, join the two head pieces leaving the seam at the neck open. Turn out.

6. Sew the felt face in place using the pattern piece as reference (see page 85). Using a double thickness of six-stranded embroidery silk, sew two French knot eyes and, with a single thickness of sewing thread, two French knot nostrils. Stitch a stem stitch mouth with three strands of embroidery silk.

7. With right sides facing, join the pairs of ears together, leaving the straight edges unstitched. Turn right side out, stuff lightly, then fold the seam allowance to the inside.

8. Hand stitch the ears onto the head referring to the photograph for position.

9. Sew the motif to one ear.

10. Pin the legs in position at the bottom seam and hand-stitch firmly in place through all layers. Hand-stitch the remaining gap at the bottom seam to close.

11. Stuff the body firmly through the neck opening. Pin the arms in position at the neck seam and hand-stitch firmly in place through layers.

12. Stuff the head firmly through the neck edge. Fold in the seam allowance at the neck edge and hand-stitch the head to the neck.

DRESS

13. The seam allowance on the dress is 3 mm ($\frac{1}{8}$ in). With right sides together, stitch the front to the back along the side seams and shoulder seams, leaving the armholes open. Turn right side out.

14. Embroider a few rows of smocking at the front and then sew the braid along the hem and around the neck.

Puppy

MATERIALS
- One adult's sock, white with black polka dots for body and legs
- Black felt scraps for ears
- Black embroidery thread
- Toy stuffing

BODY

1. With right sides together, sew the body seam, leaving a gap for stuffing.

2. Turn right side out, stuff, then sew the gap to close.

3. Sew on the felt ears and embroider facial features.

LEGS

4. With right sides together, stitch the leg seams, leaving the top straight edge open. Turn right side out and stuff. Fold in seam allowance and sew to the pup's belly.

Tweetle Turtle

Slow and steady wins the race. Turtles and tortoises are so appealing, with their little beady eyes and friendly expressions – I hope I've done them justice with my cuddly, tactile toy. Since rough linen fabric frays beautifully, I used it for the shell to create the fluffy edge on each of the patchwork pieces.

MATERIALS
- Green linen: 50 cm (20 in), 112 cm (45 in) wide for upper shell. (Alternatively: use white linen and tie-dye with green machine dye and elastic bands.)
- Cotton fabric: 50 cm (20 in) square for base of shell, back, belly, legs, tail, head
- Two small black beads
- Brown, white, orange and green felt scraps
- Olive or brown embroidery thread for facial features and claws
- Toy stuffing

Templates:
See pages 82-83.

DYEING LINEN
1. Twist the elastic bands randomly over the linen. This will produce a tie-dyed effect. Dye the fabric following the manufacturer's guidelines. When dry, remove the bands.

SHELL

2. After cutting out the templates, lay out the large hexagons in two rows radiating around a single central hexagon.

3. Join the hexagons with wrong sides together, so that the seam allowance is visible on the right side of the shell, stitching along each adjacent edge. The edge will become fluffy of its own accord, although you may wish to trim it a bit.

4. Sew small felted hexagons to medium sized ones. Hand-sew them to the shell.

5. Using the pattern for the shell, transfer the shape to the right side of the patchwork and cut out the upper shell.

6. With right sides together, stitch the upper shell to the base of the shell, leaving a gap for stuffing. Turn right side out. Stuff the shell, then stitch gap to close.

LEGS

7. With right sides together, join the seams of the two back legs, leaving the straight edges at the top open. Turn right side out and stuff lightly.

8. With right sides together, join the seams of each front leg, leaving the straight edge at the top open. Turn right side out.

9. Stitch the claws to the outside of the foot end of the front legs. Stuff the front legs.

BODY AND HEAD

10. With right sides together, join the seams of the head and the tail, leaving the straight edges at the top open. Turn right side out and stuff lightly.

11. With right sides together, join the back to the belly, at the same time catching in the four legs, tail and the head, leaving a gap for stuffing. Turn right side out through the gap, stuff firmly and stitch the gap shut (the legs and tail should hang out from the side seams).

12. Fix the shell to the turtle's back by catching the underside of the shell to the back at various points, and to the neck, which allows for the head to look upward.

DETAILS

13. Stitch the white of the eye to each side of the head.

14. Sew on a bead to represent the iris of the eye.

15. Using three strands of embroidery thread, work a French knot for nostrils. Sew a line to represent the mouth.

Smart Bear

This traditional teddy is one of my favourite projects as he makes a great heirloom piece to pass down from generation to generation. His robust linen body and strong button joints provide a nice contrast to his gingham paws and a patchwork heart.

MATERIALS
- Natural colour linen: 1 m (1 yd) square
- Yellow gingham fabric for front paws, ears, back of head, bow, back foot pads
- Brown and red felt scraps for nose and heart motif
- Cream and black embroidery thread for facial features
- Brown 4-ply yarn for claws
- 4 buttons for joints
- Two buttons for eyes
- Strong button thread
- Toy stuffing or scraps of material to use as stuffing

Templates:
See page 86.

LEGS AND ARMS
1. With right sides together, stitch the seams of each leg, leaving the top and bottom edges open.
2. With right sides together, stitch the footpads to the bottom of the legs, matching the large and small dots. Clip the curves and turn the legs right side out.
3. Stuff the legs firmly until close to the top. Turn the seam allowance at the top to the inside, add a small amount of stuffing at the top and slipstitch to close.
4. With right sides together, sew a paw pad to each inner and outer arm.
5. With right sides together, stitch each entire arm together, leaving a gap in the back seam for turning and stuffing.
6. Turn right side out, stuff and close seam as for the legs.

BODY
7. Stitch darts in the body pieces at the bear's posterior and neck edge. With right

sides together, stitch the body seam, leaving neck edge open.

8. Stuff the body and turn in the seam allowance around the neck.

EARS

9. With right sides together, stitch each pair of ear pieces along the outer curve, leaving the straight edge open. Clip the curves and turn right side out. Stuff and tack the straight edges together to close the gap.

HEAD

10. With right sides together, stitch the head front pieces together along the centre line. Turn right side out.

11. Position the ears on the head front.

12. With right sides together, stitch the head fronts to the head back, catching in the ears as you do so and leaving the neck edge open. Clip the curves, turn right side out and stuff firmly.

13. Position the head in the neck opening of the body and slipstitch the edges together securely.

FEATURES

14. Thread a needle with black embroidery thread and knot one end. Insert the needle into the nose area and bring it out at a mouth corner, then insert the yarn at the other edge of the mouth, allowing the yarn to lie loosely as a smile. Bring the thread out in the centre of the mouth and make a small backstitch to hold the mouth in place. Secure the thread back in the nose area.

15. Sew on the felt nose with cream embroidery thread and sew on two button eyes.

16. Using cream embroidery thread, sew the heart to bear's chest with small blanket stitches.

17. Using a strip of gingham fabric, tie a bow around teddy's neck.

JOINING LIMBS

18. With strong button thread, sew a large button to each of the arms near the top edge and then take the thread through to the body at the arm position. Sew securely in place. Sew the legs to the body in the same way.

19. Use the brown yarn to stitch four claws on each foot, two either side of the centre front seam.

Felty Dinosaurs

These immortal giants are bought to life here in fun, felty technicolour and when your small fry is done with playtime, simply stash these pint-sized creatures in the egg-shaped bag. Re-create your very own Jurassic park with felted favourites such as the Stegosaurus and the fierce T-Rex.

T-Rex

MATERIALS

- Felt: two x 30 x 15 cm (12 x 6 in) pieces in red for body; 30 x 15 cm (12 x 6 in) piece in maroon for outer hind legs; 30 x 15 cm (12 x 6 in) piece, brown for underside of body; green scraps for inner hind legs, front legs; orange scrap for mouth
- White, black, coloured embroidery silks for details

Templates:
See page 87.

Note:

Work with three strands of embroidery silk throughout.

BODY

1. Place the wrong side of the throat/chest pieces on the right side of each body piece and embroider in position. Take front legs and embroider the shoulders in position on body, leaving the legs to flap free.

2. Place the pieces for the underside of the tail on each body piece and embroider them into position.

3. Use blanket stitch to stitch from dot to dot around the end of the tail, up the backbone, around the head, down the throat and across the chest.

HIND LEGS

4. Join each outer leg to its inner leg between the dots, using blanket stitch.

5. Stitch the outer legs to the body.

STUFFING

6. Stuff the head, body, legs and tail using a pencil to pack the stuffing in firmly.

7. Stitch the underbelly in place between the inner legs, working short, stabbing backstitches, packing the stuffing in as tightly as you can as you close the body.

8. Join the two parts of the underside of the tail with blanket stitch.

DETAILS

9. Make each eye by working a French knot.

10. Join each mouth piece to the head with small stitches. Join at the centre with blanket stitch. Using white embroidery silk and long stitches, work a zigzag of teeth around mouth.

11. Use French knots to sew evenly spaced discs along the backbone.

Stegosaurus

MATERIALS

- Felt: 30 x 15 cm (12 x 6 in) piece, mid-brown for body and outer legs; 30 x 15 cm (12 x 6 in) piece, yellow for underbelly; 30 x 15 cm (12 x 6 in) piece, olive green for spinal plates
- Black, coloured embroidery silks for detail

Templates:
See page 88.

Note:
Work with three strands of embroidery silk throughout.

BODY

1. Place the wrong side of the two underbelly pieces on the right side of each body piece. Work short horizontal stitches over the join.
2. Stitch discs randomly over the body.
3. Tack the spinal plates piece in position on the wrong side of one body piece.
4. With wrong sides together, stitch the two halves of the body together from dot to dot, stitching around the head, backbone and tail with short, stabbing stitches. Catch in the spinal plates piece along the backbone as you go.

LEGS

5. Place the wrong side of the outer legs on the right side of the body and stitch in place between the dots, again with short horizontal stitches.
6. Join the outer leg to the inner leg, from dot to dot, using blanket stitch. Repeat with other leg.

STUFFING

7. Stuff the body, head and legs, using a pencil to pack the stuffing in firmly.
8. Close the underside of the body with blanket stitch, drawing each pair of legs together and eliminating gaps.

FACE

9. Work a French knot for each eye and backstitch a mouth.

Baby Stegosaurus and Egg

MATERIALS

- Felt: 30 x 15 cm (12 x 6 in), piece, lime for body; scrap green for spinal plates; scrap yellow for spots; two x 15 cm (6 in) bright pink square pieces for eggshell; 15 cm (6 in) light pink square for interior of egg and spots
- Black, coloured embroidery silks for detail

Templates:
See page 88.

Note:
Work with three strands of embroidery silk throughout.

BABY STEGOSAURUS

1. Stitch spots randomly over both body pieces, securing them with a French knot.
2. Tack the spinal plates piece in position on the wrong side of one body piece.
3. With wrong sides together, stitch body pieces together along the head, backbone and

around the tail and legs, working short, stabbing stitches. Catch in the spinal plates as you do so and leave a gap for stuffing. Stuff lightly and continue the stitching to close the gap.

4. Embroider the facial features: work a French knot for each eye and backstitch a mouth with black thread.

EGG

1. Sew pink spots randomly over the eggshell by working a French knot in the centre.

2. With wrong sides together, place the front eggshell pieces over the interior of the egg, matching edges. Tack together.

3. With wrong sides together, place the front and back eggshell together and stitch the edges with blanket stitch through all three layers, leaving a gap for stuffing. Stuff lightly through the gap and then close the opening with blanket stitch.

4. Remove the tacking stitches.

Brontosaurus

MATERIALS

- Felt: two x 30 x 15 cm (12 x 6 in) pieces, turquoise for body/head, outer legs; one piece, 30 x 15 cm (12 x 6 in), blue for underbelly, spots; one piece, 15 cm (6 in) square for inner legs; scraps light blue for oval spots
- Black, coloured embroidery silks for detail

Templates:
See page 87.

Note:
Work with three strands of embroidery silk throughout.

BODY

1. Place the wrong side of the two underbelly pieces on the right side of each body piece. Work short horizontal stitches over the join.

2. Stitch round and oval spots randomly over the body.

3. With wrong sides together, use blanket stitch to sew the two halves of the body together from dot to dot,

stitching under the chin and around the head, backbone and tail.

LEGS

4. Place the wrong side of the outer legs on the right side of the body and stitch in place between the dots, again with short horizontal stitches.

5. Join the outer leg to the inner leg on both legs, from dot to dot, using blanket stitch.

STUFFING

6. Stuff the body, head and legs, using a pencil to pack the stuffing in firmly.

7. Close the underside of the body with blanket stitch, drawing each pair of legs together and eliminating gaps.

FACE

8. Work a French knot for each eye and backstitch a mouth.

Pterodactyl

MATERIALS

- Felt: 30 x 15 cm (12 x 6 in) piece, dark pink for back head/wings; 30 x 15 cm (12 x 6 in) piece, mauve for front wings; 15 cm (6 in) square, white for body front
- Black, coloured embroidery silks for detail

Templates:
See page 88-89.

Note:

Work with three strands of embroidery silk throughout.

MAKING UP

1. With wrong side of body front to right side of front wings, stitch under the arms and down side using white thread and short horizontal stitches. Work random stitches across body front to attach to the wings.
2. With wrong side to wrong side, stitch body front to back, working blanket stitch around the head and wings and leaving a gap for stuffing. Stuff lightly, then continue the blanket stitch to close the gap.
3. Work a French knot for each eye and backstitch a mouth.

Egg bag

MATERIALS

- Blue fleece: two x 43 x 30 cm (17 x 12 in) for front and back; 105 x 10 cm (42 x 4 in) for gusset
- Felt scraps for spots
- Coloured embroidery silks for detail
- 33 cm (13 in) zipper
- Small amounts of toy stuffing for spots

Template:
See page 89.

GUSSET

1. With right sides together, join the seams of the gusset. Cut a slit in the gusset between the dots, ending in two V-shaped slits (see diagram). The slit should be 2.5 cm (1 in) shorter, at each end, than the length of the zipper.
2. At the edges around the slit, turn 6 mm (¼ in) to the wrong side and tack in place. Tack the zip in position and then sew in place. Open the zipper.

FRONT AND BACK

3. With right sides together, pin and then tack the front to the gusset. Machine sew the seam. Repeat for the back.
4. Turn right side out through the open zipper.

SPOTS

5. Stitch each spot to the bag with a line of running stitch around the perimeter, leaving an opening for stuffing. Insert a tiny amount of stuffing and complete the stitching.

Pull-Along Nellie

A spotty, eye-catching, squidgy elephant toy. Make her with or without the wheeled base. (The base could also be used for other animals in the book: just adjust the size to suit.)

MATERIALS

Elephant
- Spotted cotton: 50 cm (20 in), 112 cm (45 in) wide for body
- Cotton scraps for ears and tail
- Felt scraps for foot pads and eyes
- Toy stuffing

Base
- Birch-faced plywood: 100 x 150 x 12 mm (4 x 6 x ½ in) for base; four circles, 3 cm (1¼ in) in diameter, 12 mm (½ in) thick for wheels
- Four 2.5 cm (1 in) screws and four cups
- Small screw-in closed hook
- String for pull-cord
- Non-toxic paint
- Sandpaper
- Strong, non-toxic fabric glue

Templates:
See page 90-91.

LEGS AND BELLY

1. With right sides together stitch the front and back inner legs to each body piece, leaving the bottom of the legs open. Turn right side out.

2. With right sides together, stitch the belly pieces along the centre seam, leaving a gap for turning. With right sides together, stitch the belly to the body between the dots. Turn under the seam allowance at bottom of legs and press.

3. With right sides together and a 3 mm (⅛ in) seam, stitch the tail pieces, leaving the short end open. Turn right side out and press flat. Tack in position on the right side of one of the body pieces.

STUFFING

4. With right sides together, stitch the seam across the top of the body, head and trunk, catching in the tail. Turn right side out.

5. Stuff the body, using a pencil to pack the stuffing into the trunk.

6. Close the gap in the underside with slipstitches. Pack the stuffing into the legs and then ease the felt foot pads to fit the lower edge of the legs. Stitch the pads to the legs with blanket stitch.

EARS AND EYES

7. With right sides together, stitch the curved seams of the ear pieces, leaving the straight edge open. Turn right side out. Turn under 6 mm (¼ in) on the straight edges and whipstitch together. Pin the ears on the head and then whipstitch in place.

8. Sew on the felt eyes with a French knot.

WHEELED BASE

1. Drill a 6 mm (¼ in) hole in the centre of each wheel. Drill two holes of the same size into sides of the wooden base at the wheel positions. Attach each wheel with a screw and cup.

2. Screw the closed hook securely to the front edge. Tie a short cord to the hook. If the toy is for a child under three years old, the cord must not be any longer than 23 cm (9 in) long, to prevent strangulation.

3. Paint the base and sand down to achieve a worn look.

4. When dry, paste glue on the bottom of the foot pads and stick the elephant on the base. Leave to dry completely.

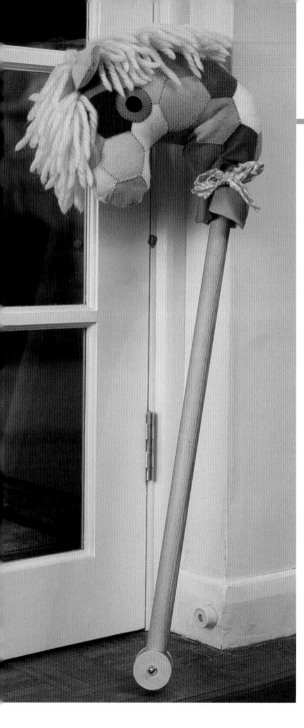

Hobby Horse

With a colourful patchwork design and a textured mane, this hobby horse will send your wee cowboy riding off into the sunset in style. If you have a pile of colourful scraps of felt, play with colours to create the patchwork – the results may just surprise you.

MATERIALS

- Felt: approx. 40 hexagons (see template)
- Felt scraps for outer and inner eyes
- Strip of fabric for tie
- Chunky yarn for mane
- Large-eyed needle
- Toy stuffing
- Broom handle or wooden curtain pole: 1 m (1 yd) long
- Strong fabric glue
- Birch-faced plywood: two circles, 5 cm (1¼ in) in diameter, 12 mm (½ in) thick for wheels
- Two 2.5 cm (1 in) screws and four cups

Templates:
See page 93.

Note:

The seam allowance throughout is 3 mm (⅛ in).

MAKING UP

1. To make one side, begin by placing hexagons right side up over your template, starting with one in the middle and working your way around it. Continue to piece as above, fitting the templates shape.

2. Position the remaining pieces to just cover the template and once satisfied with arrangement, sew the pieces in place.

3. Trace the the template on the patchwork fabric and cut out the shape.

4. Repeat steps 1-3 with other side of head.

5. Sew on eyes, using photograph and the pattern for correct placement.

6. With right sides together, sew around the head of horse, leaving the neck edge open.

Trim and snip seam allowance along the curved lines. Turn right side out.

7. With wrong sides together, sew the ears, leaving the straight edge open. Stuff lightly, then sew gap to close.

8. Stitch the ears to the top of the head at the seamline.

9. To attach mane, cut a length of yarn to the length of the top of the nose to halfway along the neck. Whipstitch it firmly across the seam at the top of the head.

10. Cut the remaining yarn into 20 cm (8 in) lengths. Attach each 'hair' to the whipstitched yarn by folding a strand in half and threading the folded end through the large-eyed needle. Push the needle through the whipstitched yarn at the top of the head, remove the needle, then pull the ends of the yarn through the loop. Pull up to lie against the whipstitched length. Work the rest of the mane along the top seam. Trim if necessary.

11. Stuff the head firmly, leaving room for the pole.

12. Apply glue on the top of

the pole, then push it into the head. Adjust the head so it is not lopsided, then leave the glue to dry. Add more stuffing if necessary. When you are happy with the head, bunch up the felt at the neck and tie securely with the frayed strip of fabric.

13. To add wheels, follow the instructions on page 59.

Cat & Mouse Skittles

The game of skittles is easy and fun for all ages and this simple-to-make version is great fun! Line up the mouse skittles and roll the cat bowling ball at them, just like a cat pouncing on its prey. The mice are sweet enough to be made as individual toys.

MATERIALS

- Felt: 20 x 10 cm (8 x 4 in) piece for mouse's body; 9 x 6 cm (3½ x 2½ in) piece for mouse's head
- Felt scraps for mice features
- Beige sewing thread for whiskers
- Grey, white, pink, black felt scraps for cat's body, ears and nose
- Black embroidery silk for cat's facial features
- Large-eyed needle
- Toy stuffing
- Scrap of thick card to reinforce base of mice

Templates:
See page 92.

Note:
The seam allowance throughout is 3 mm (⅛ in).

Mouse

MAKING UP

1. With right sides together, sew the head to the body at the neck edge.

2. With right sides together, fold the body in half lengthways and stitch along the head and body seam, leaving the straight base edge open. Clip the felt close to the stitches and clip the corner at the nose end.

STUFFING

3. Turn right side out and stuff, using a pencil to push the stuffing into the nose and pack down firmly. Holding the mouse upside down, insert the cardboard disc into the base so that it is even with the lower edge of the body. Place more stuffing around the disc but not on top of it.

TAIL

4. Cut a strip of felt 20 cm x 12 mm (8 x ½ in). With wrong sides together, fold tail in half, whipstitch the edges together.

5. Place the end of the tail on the wrong side of the bottom of the centre back seam. Tack in place. Pin the felt base to the lower edge of the body, easing the body to fit. Using two strands of cotton thread, whipstitch the base in place, catching in the tail and covering the cardboard disc.

EARS AND EYES

6. Fold each ear in half and stitch to the head across the pleat line at the bottom edge. If desired, sew a motif between the ears or on body.

7. Sew the eyes to the head by working a French knot in the centre of each felt disc.

WHISKERS

8. Cut a double strand of cotton thread approximately 7.5 cm (3 in) long. Make each whisker by folding the double strand in half and threading the folded end through a

sewing needle. Pass the needle through the nose, take the needle out and pull the ends of the thread through the loop of yarn. Pull up so the loop lies against the felt. Trim the whiskers if necessary. Sew three or four whiskers to each side of the nose.

9. Make five or more mice, you can play with the colours.

Cat bowling ball

MAKING UP

1. Sew the facial features and the ears on one of the segments. The eyes are two French knots and the mouth consists of three straight stitches. Overcast the edges of the nose and the ears.

2. With right sides together, whipstitch the segments together, sewing two long sides in pairs to make two cups. Join the two cups with whipstitch, one side with a vertical seam and the other with a horizontal seam, leaving a gap large enough for turning and stuffing.

3. Turn right side out and stuff firmly. Stitch the gap to close.

Bears in Waistcoats

Peekaboo! These cute, cheeky bear necessities are simple enough for children to enjoy sewing and they're also quick to make for craft fairs or stocking fillers. Create them in your favourite colours.

MATERIALS

- Felt: two x 30 x 15 cm (12 x 6 in) pieces for body of each bear
- Felt scraps for muzzle and waistcoat
- Black seed beads for eyes
- Black embroidery silk for facial features
- Toy stuffing

Templates:
See page 94.

Note:
The seam allowance throughout is 3 mm (1/8 in).

BODY
1. With right sides together, pin the front body to the back body. Stitch around the bear, leaving a gap at the side between the dots.
2. Trim about 2 mm (1/16 in) from the seam.
3. Stuff the bear, packing the stuffing into the ears, arms and legs. Turn the seam allowance around the gap to the inside and slipstitch the gap to close it.

FACE
4. Place the muzzle on the face and whipstitch the edges, leaving a small gap. Stuff lightly through the gap and

then complete the sewing around the muzzle.

5. With three strands of embroidery silk, satin stitch the nose and sew lines for the mouth. Take the needle and thread up through the back of the muzzle and bring it out at the position of one of the eyes. Sew on a bead securely. Repeat for the other eye.

6. To accentuate the shape of the bear's head, stitch around the outline of the head, through all layers, about 3 mm (1/8 in) from the edge and across the bottom of the face. Use a thread in the same colour as the felt and a running stitch. Stitch another line across the base of the ears.

WAISTCOAT

7. Butt the side seam edges of the waistcoat against each other and whipstitch together. (If you wish, you could decorate the waistcoat with beads or felt motifs.)

Retro Tea Set

With this totally unbreakable, squishy-squashy retro tea set, role-playing can be done in real style. And no tea party would be complete without snacks – these felted gingerbread men are almost good enough to eat.

MATERIALS

- Felt: 30 x 15 cm (12 x 6 in) piece for tea pot sides; 15 cm (6 in) square for lid; two x 8 cm (3¼ in) circles for base and knob on lid; 3 x 16 cm (1¼ x 6¼ in) piece for handle; 12 cm (4¾ in) square for spout
- Felt scraps for cups, saucers, gingerbread men
- Sequins
- Ricrac braid: 30 cm (12 in) per saucer
- Black beads or buttons for gingerbread men's eyes
- Toy stuffing
- PVA glue

Templates:
See page 95.

Note:
The seam allowance throughout is 3 mm (⅛ in) unless directed otherwise.

Tea pot

SIDES
1. With the right side uppermost, roll up the piece for the tea pot sides so that the back seam overlaps by 2.5 cm (1 in). Hand-sew to join.

LID
2. With the right side uppermost, join the seam on the lid by lapping one edge over the other, following the given seam allowance. With wrong sides together, pinch together the sides of the tea pot with the lid and join with whipstitch.

3. Take the piece for the knob on the lid and run a gathering stitch around the outside. Pull up slightly and fill with stuffing. Draw up the thread tightly and secure. Sew the knob to the top of the lid.

SPOUT

4. With the wrong side inside, bring together the long edges of the spout and whipstitch. Referring to the photograph for positioning, join the wrong side of the spout to the right side of the tea pot, working running stitch 3 mm (1/8 in) in from where they meet. You may wish to tack this in place first, as it can be a little tricky.

STUFFING

5. Stuff the pot and lid through the base of the pot, allowing the stuffing to go into the base of the spout. Pinch together the wrong side of the base and the wrong side of the tea pot and join with whipstitch.

HANDLE

6. With the wrong side inside, lap one long edge of the strip over the other. Work a short stabbing stitch to join.

7. Sew the ends of the handle to the pot, with the lower end about 2.5 cm (1 in) from the bottom of the pot. (Place the handle seam on the inside and position over the seam of the tea pot sides.)

8. Glue sequins to the sides of the tea pot.

Tea cups

MAKING UP

1. With the right side uppermost, roll up the piece for the cup sides so that the back seam overlaps the given allowance. Hand-sew to join.

2. With wrong sides together, pinch together the base and sides of the cup/jug and join with whipstitch.

3. Make and attach the handles as for tea pot.

4. Glue on the sequins.

5. Join the two pieces for each saucer with a running stitch around the edge. On the upper side of the saucer, sew ricrac over the stitching.

Gingerbread men

MAKING UP

1. Cut out the shapes and then sew on bead eyes and buttons using tiny backstitches.

Little felt houses

Children love secret drawers and trinket boxes and these houses are actually little pockets for children to hang off bedposts, shelves or wherever they choose. Make a home for tiny dolls and animals, stash hidden treasures or conceal favourite sweets!

MATERIALS

- Felt: two x 30 x 15 cm (12 x 6 in) pieces, for walls, base and roof, per house
- Felt scraps in assorted colours for pelmet, window and motif
- Gingham scraps for curtains; 18 mm x 28 cm (¾ x 11 in) for hanging loop
- Narrow ribbon or embroidery thread for curtain and door ties

Template:
See page 71.

Note:

The seam allowance throughout is 3 mm (⅛ in).

ROOF

1. Make the hanging loop. Take each piece and fold the seam allowance to the inside. Whipstitch the edges together. If desired, finish one end by poking the edges to the inside and whipstitch in place. Tack the finished pieces to the right side of the top of the roof, with the raw edges at the top.
2. With right sides together, sew the seam in the roof to form a cone, catching in the pieces for the hanging loop. Turn right side out.

WALLS

3. With wrong side of the pelmet to the right side of wall, sew in place.
4. Roll the wall piece around and lap one edge over the other, adjusting so the cone roof will fit. Whipstitch the back seam of the wall. Fit the cone to the top of the main house and whipstitch in place.
5. Ease in the base and whipstitch in place.

WINDOW AND DOOR

6. Sew the cross-pieces of the window frame behind the windows.

7. Hem the curtains around all the raw edges. Stitch the top edge above the window. Thread the ribbon tie through the wall just above the window. Roll up the curtain and tie with the ribbon.
8. Make a vertical cut to establish each side of the door. Thread the other ribbon tie through the wall above the door. Roll up the door and secure with the ribbon.
9. Sew on flowers or motifs.

Templates

- - - - - - - -	sewing line
——————	cutting line
——————	pattern placement
△	notches
←——————	grainline
•	match points
··················	join pattern before cutting

Little Felt Houses
(page 68)

Enlarge all
templates
on this page
to 200%.

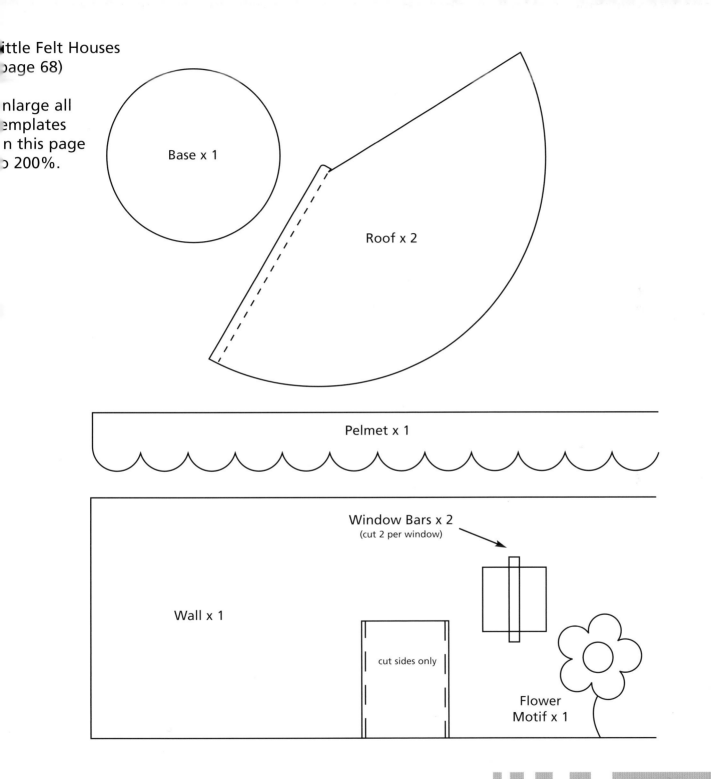

Base x 1

Roof x 2

Pelmet x 1

Window Bars x 2
(cut 2 per window)

Wall x 1

cut sides only

Flower
Motif x 1

**Basic Doll
(page 14)**

Enlarge all
templates
on this
page to
200%.

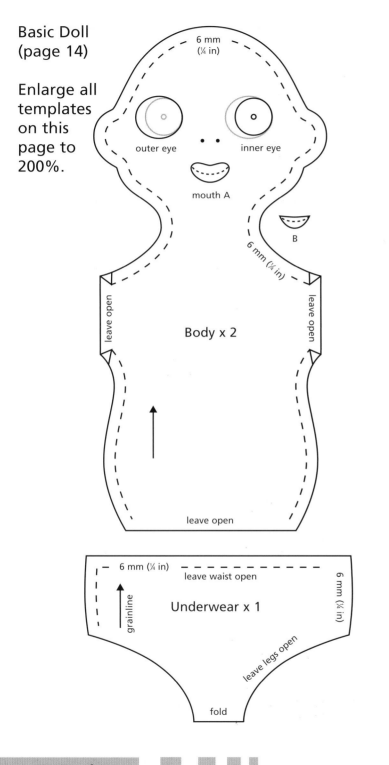

6 mm
(¼ in)

outer eye

inner eye

mouth A

B

6 mm (¼ in)

leave open

leave open

Body x 2

leave open

6 mm (¼ in)

leave waist open

grainline

Underwear x 1

6 mm (¼ in)

leave legs open

fold

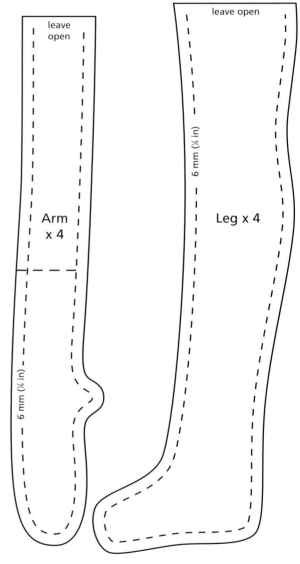

leave open

leave open

Arm
x 4

6 mm (¼ in)

Leg x 4

6 mm (¼ in)

asic Shoes
imple Trousers
leeveless Top
page 17)

nlarge all templates on
his page to 200%.

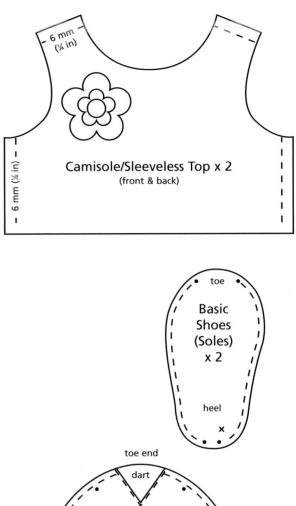

Camisole/Sleeveless Top x 2
(front & back)

6 mm (¼ in)

6 mm (¼ in)

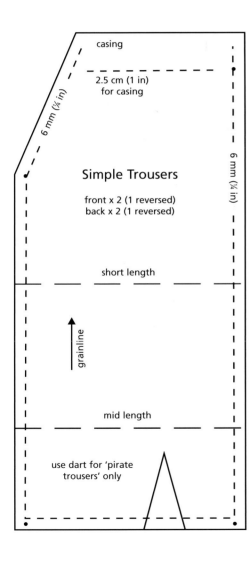

casing

2.5 cm (1 in)
for casing

6 mm (⅛ in)

6 mm (⅛ in)

Simple Trousers

front x 2 (1 reversed)
back x 2 (1 reversed)

short length

grainline

mid length

use dart for 'pirate
trousers' only

toe

**Basic
Shoes
(Soles)
x 2**

heel

×

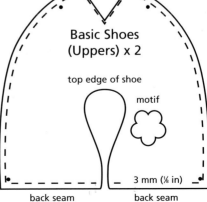

toe end

dart

**Basic Shoes
(Uppers) x 2**

top edge of shoe

motif

3 mm (⅛ in)

back seam

back seam

Basic/Mini Skirt Fur Vest and Sock (page 19)

Enlarge all templates on this page to 200%.

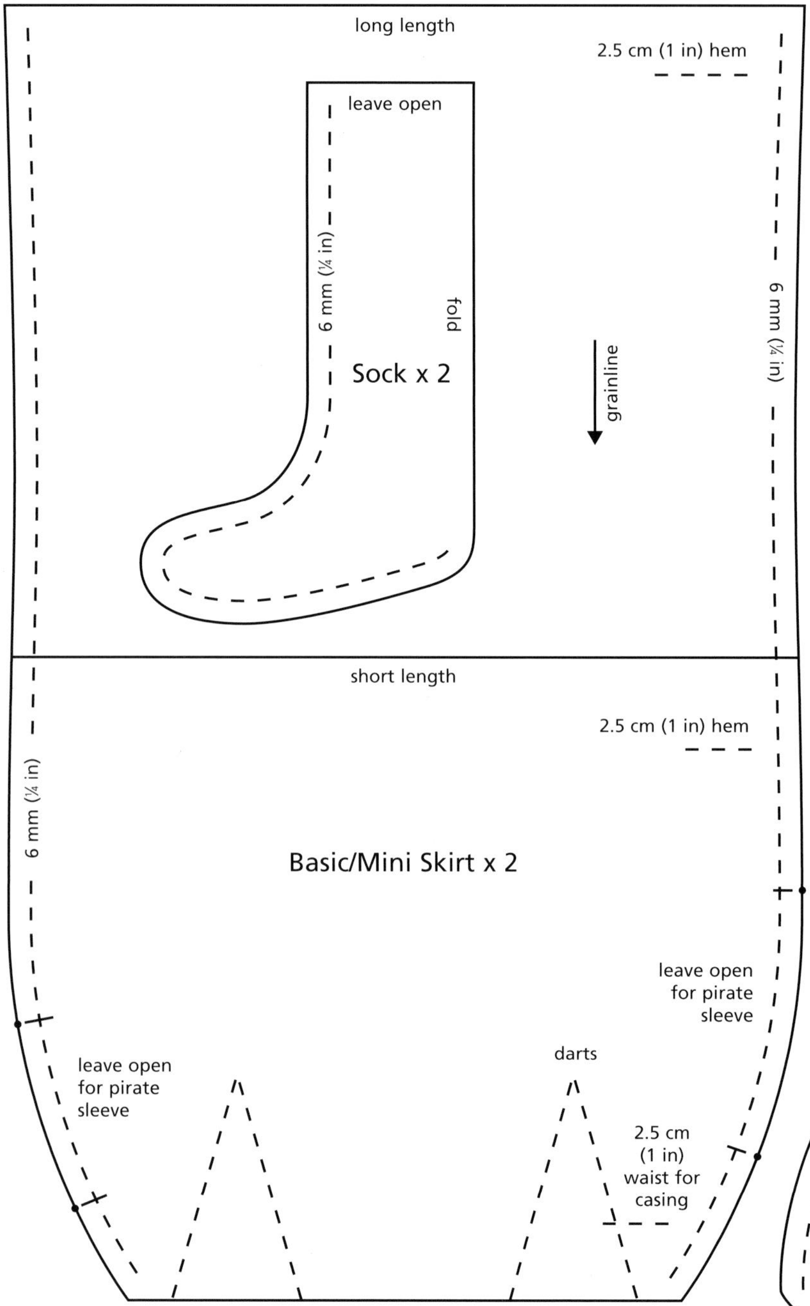

long length

2.5 cm (1 in) hem

leave open

6 mm (¼ in)

fold

Sock x 2

grainline

6 mm (¼ in)

short length

2.5 cm (1 in) hem

6 mm (¼ in)

Basic/Mini Skirt x 2

leave open for pirate sleeve

leave open for pirate sleeve

darts

2.5 cm (1 in) waist for casing

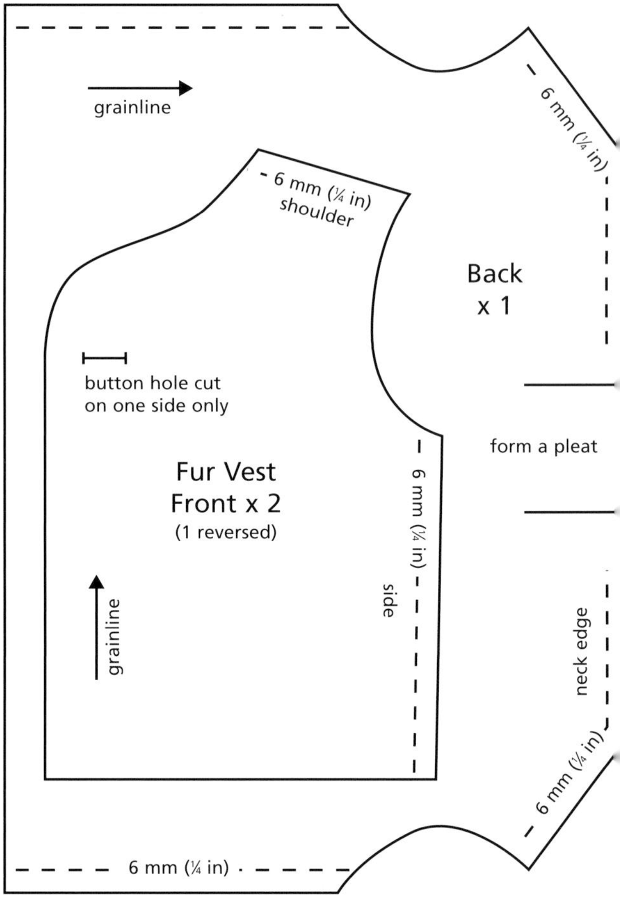

grainline

6 mm (¼ in) shoulder

button hole cut on one side only

Fur Vest Front x 2 (1 reversed)

grainline

6 mm (¼ in)

side

Back x 1

6 mm (¼ in)

form a pleat

neck edge

6 mm (¼ in)

6 mm (¼ in)

6 mm (¼ in)

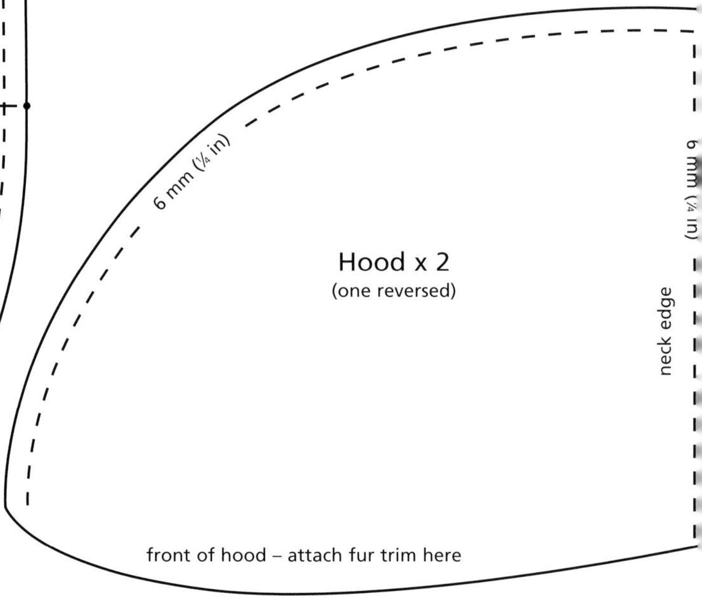

Hood x 2 (one reversed)

6 mm (¼ in)

neck edge

front of hood – attach fur trim here

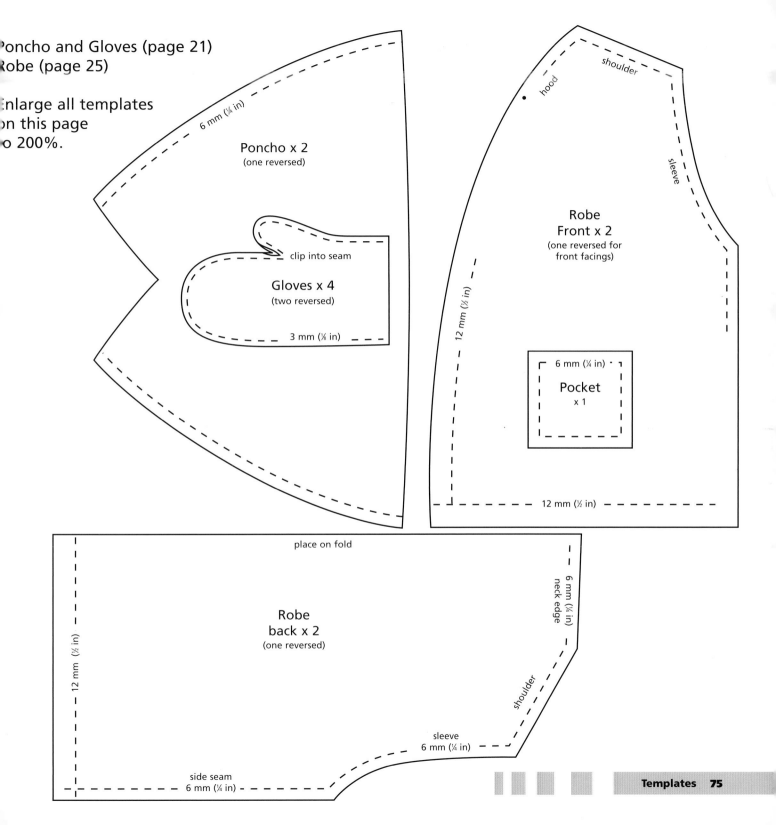

Poncho and Gloves (page 21)
Robe (page 25)

Enlarge all templates
on this page
to 200%.

Poncho x 2
(one reversed)

6 mm (¼ in)

clip into seam

Gloves x 4
(two reversed)

3 mm (⅛ in)

hood

shoulder

sleeve

Robe
Front x 2
(one reversed for
front facings)

12 mm (½ in)

6 mm (¼ in)

Pocket
x 1

12 mm (½ in)

place on fold

6 mm (¼ in)
neck edge

Robe
back x 2
(one reversed)

12 mm (½ in)

shoulder

sleeve
6 mm (¼ in)

side seam
6 mm (¼ in)

Nightclothes (page 23)
Robe (page 25)

Enlarge all templates
on this page to 200%.

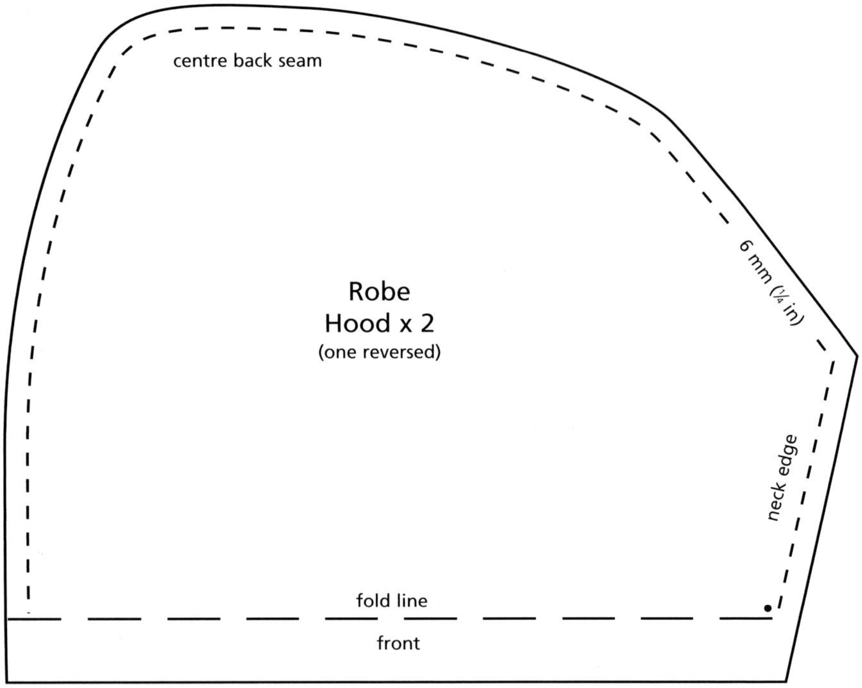

centre back seam

Robe
Hood x 2
(one reversed)

6 mm (¼ in)

neck edge

fold line

front

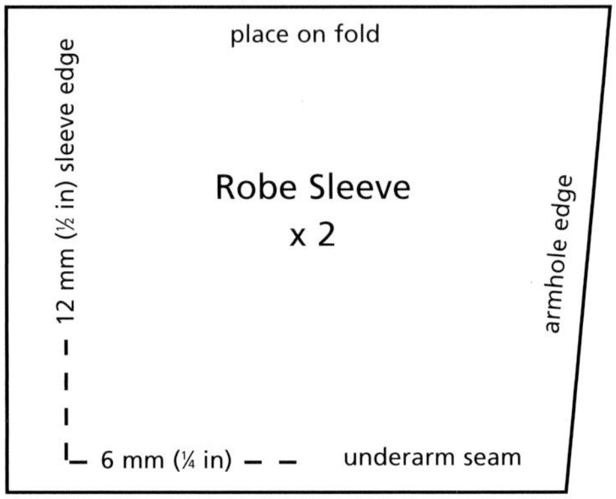

Robe Sleeve
x 2

place on fold

12 mm (½ in) sleeve edge

armhole edge

6 mm (¼ in)   underarm seam

Bunny Ear for
Slippers x 2

Pajama Top

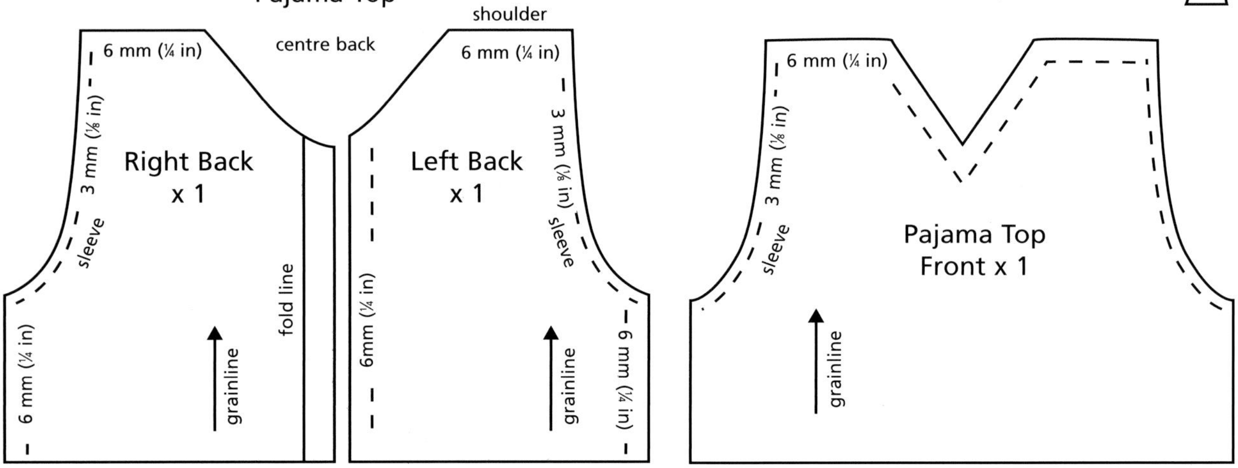

centre back

shoulder

6 mm (¼ in)

6 mm (¼ in)

3 mm (⅛ in)

sleeve

Right Back
x 1

6 mm (¼ in)

fold line

grainline

3 mm (⅛ in)

sleeve

Left Back
x 1

6mm (¼ in)

grainline

6 mm (¼ in)

6 mm (¼ in)

3 mm (⅛ in)

sleeve

Pajama Top
Front x 1

grainline

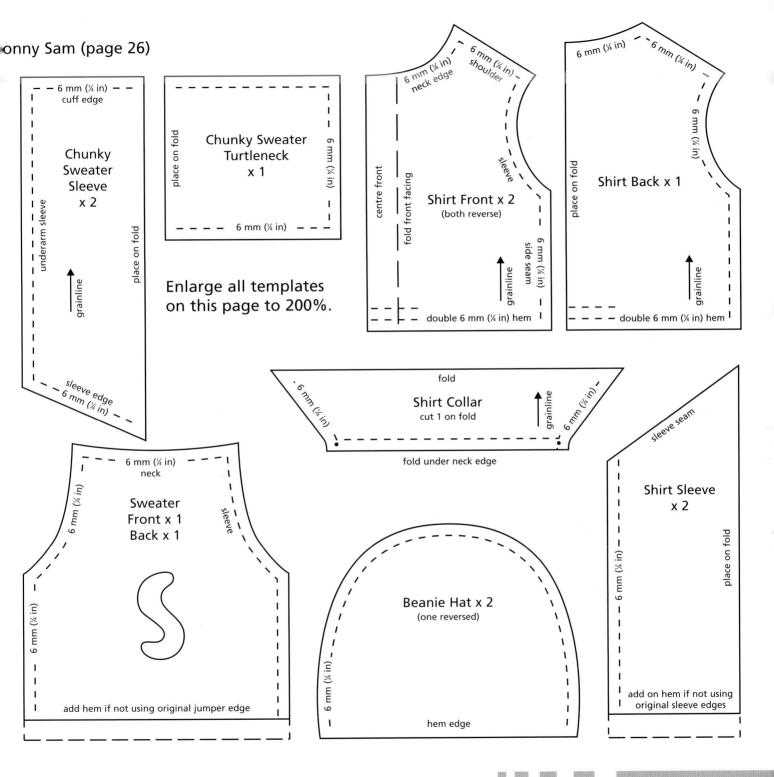

6 mm (¼ in)
cuff edge

Chunky
Sweater
Sleeve
x 2

underarm sleeve

place on fold

grainline

sleeve edge
6 mm (¼ in)

place on fold

Chunky Sweater
Turtleneck
x 1

6 mm (¼ in)

6 mm (¼ in)

Enlarge all templates
on this page to 200%.

6 mm (¼ in)
neck edge

6 mm (¼ in)
shoulder

centre front

fold front facing

Shirt Front x 2
(both reverse)

sleeve

grainline

6 mm (¼ in)
side seam

double 6 mm (¼ in) hem

6 mm (¼ in)

6 mm (¼ in)

6 mm (¼ in)

place on fold

Shirt Back x 1

grainline

double 6 mm (¼ in) hem

6 mm (¼ in)
neck

6 mm (¼ in)

Sweater
Front x 1
Back x 1

sleeve

6 mm (¼ in)

add hem if not using original jumper edge

fold

6 mm (¼ in)

Shirt Collar
cut 1 on fold

grainline

6 mm (¼ in)

fold under neck edge

Beanie Hat x 2
(one reversed)

6 mm (¼ in)

hem edge

sleeve seam

Shirt Sleeve
x 2

6 mm (¼ in)

place on fold

add on hem if not using
original sleeve edges

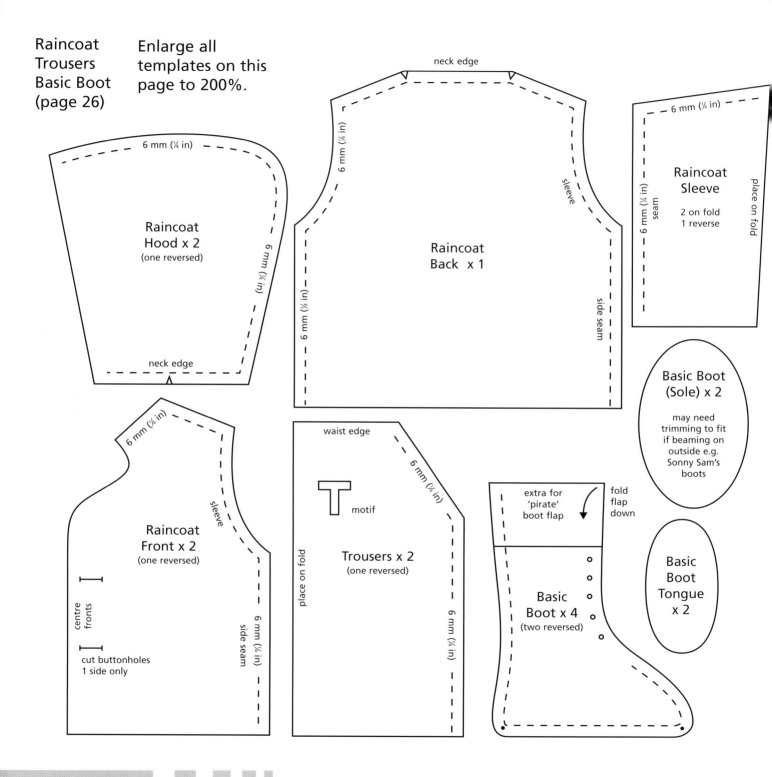

Raincoat
Trousers
Basic Boot
(page 26)

Enlarge all
templates on this
page to 200%.

neck edge

6 mm (¼ in)

Raincoat
Hood x 2
(one reversed)

6 mm (¼ in)

neck edge

6 mm (¼ in)

sleeve

Raincoat
Back x 1

side seam

6 mm (¼ in)

Raincoat
Sleeve

2 on fold
1 reverse

6 mm (¼ in)
seam

place on fold

Basic Boot
(Sole) x 2

may need
trimming to fit
if beaming on
outside e.g.
Sonny Sam's
boots

6 mm (¼ in)

sleeve

Raincoat
Front x 2
(one reversed)

centre
fronts

cut buttonholes
1 side only

6 mm (¼ in)
side seam

waist edge

6 mm (¼ in)

T motif

place on fold

Trousers x 2
(one reversed)

6 mm (¼ in)

extra for
'pirate'
boot flap

fold
flap
down

Basic
Boot x 4
(two reversed)

Basic
Boot
Tongue
x 2

Enlarge all templates
on this page to 200%.

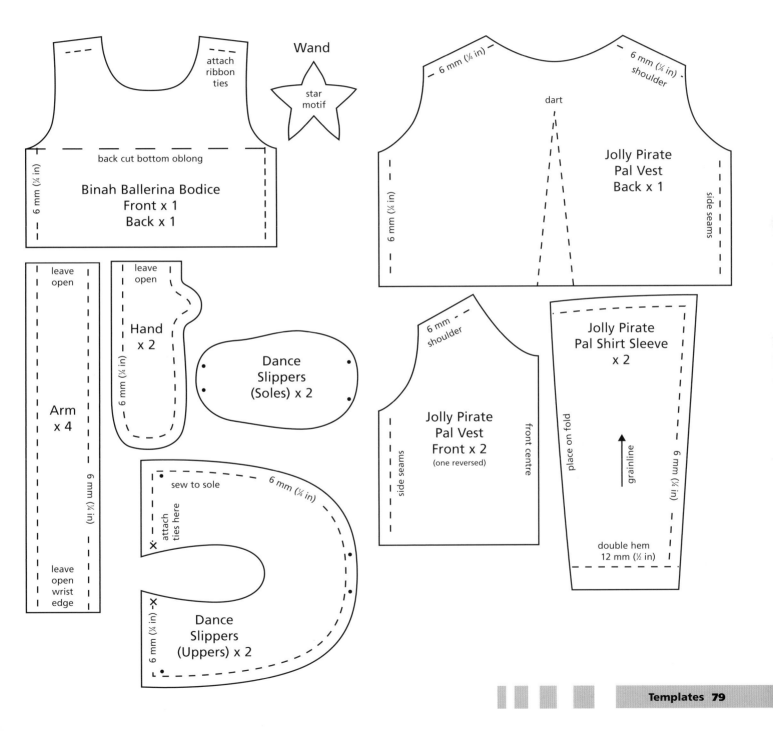

Wand
star motif

attach ribbon ties

6 mm (¼ in)

back cut bottom oblong

Binah Ballerina Bodice
Front x 1
Back x 1

6 mm (¼ in)   shoulder

6 mm (¼ in)   shoulder

dart

Jolly Pirate
Pal Vest
Back x 1

6 mm (¼ in)

side seams

leave open

leave open

Hand
x 2

6 mm (¼ in)

Dance
Slippers
(Soles) x 2

Arm
x 4

6 mm (¼ in)

6 mm shoulder

place on fold

grainline

Jolly Pirate
Pal Shirt Sleeve
x 2

6 mm (¼ in)

leave open wrist edge

sew to sole

6 mm (¼ in)

attach ties here

6 mm (¼ in)

Dance
Slippers
(Uppers) x 2

Jolly Pirate
Pal Vest
Front x 2
(one reversed)

side seams

front centre

double hem
12 mm (½ in)

Pink Elephant (page 38)

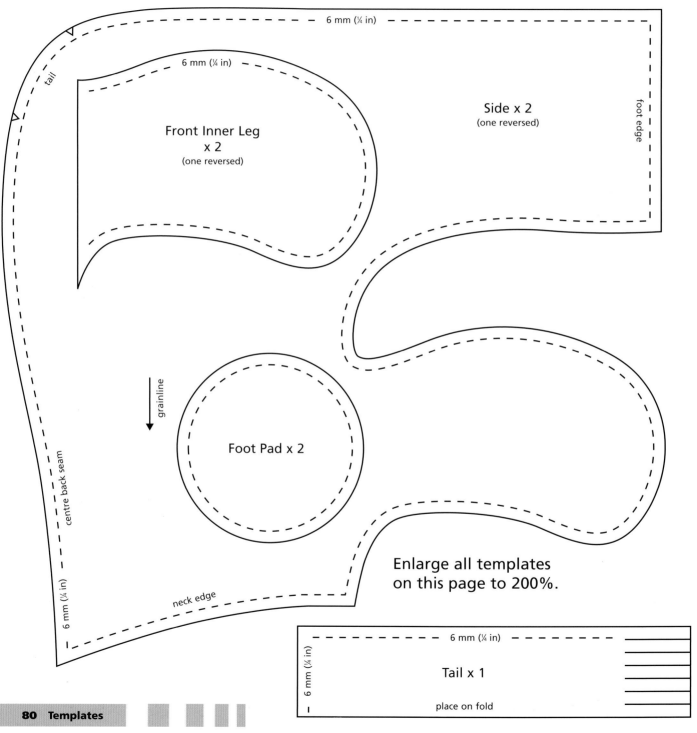

6 mm (¼ in)

tail

6 mm (¼ in)

Front Inner Leg
x 2
(one reversed)

Side x 2
(one reversed)

foot edge

grainline

centre back seam

Foot Pad x 2

Enlarge all templates
on this page to 200%.

6 mm (¼ in)

neck edge

6 mm (¼ in)

6 mm (¼ in)

Tail x 1

place on fold

outlines for tail fringe

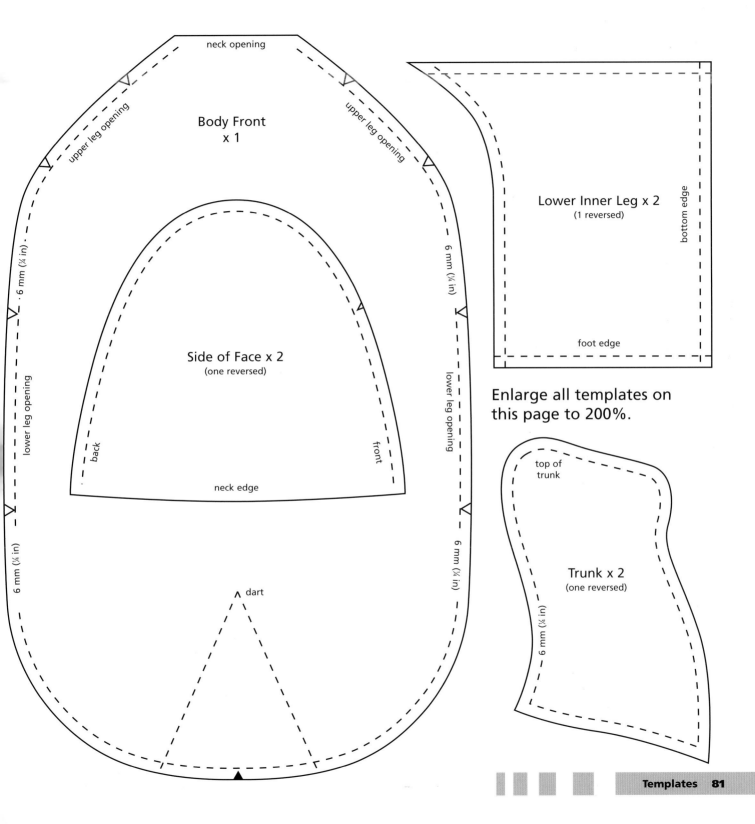

neck opening

Body Front
x 1

upper leg opening

upper leg opening

6 mm (¼ in)

6 mm (¼ in)

Side of Face x 2
(one reversed)

back

front

neck edge

lower leg opening

lower leg opening

6 mm (¼ in)

6 mm (¼ in)

dart

Lower Inner Leg x 2
(1 reversed)

bottom edge

foot edge

Enlarge all templates on
this page to 200%.

top of
trunk

Trunk x 2
(one reversed)

6 mm (¼ in)

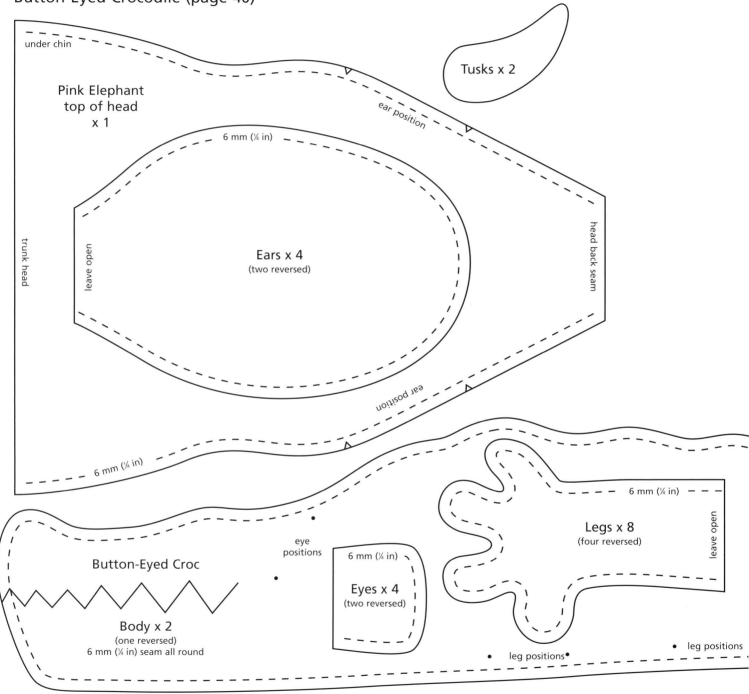

under chin

Pink Elephant
top of head
x 1

6 mm (¼ in)

Tusks x 2

ear position

Ears x 4
(two reversed)

leave open

trunk head

head back seam

6 mm (¼ in)

ear position

6 mm (¼ in)

6 mm (¼ in)

Legs x 8
(four reversed)

leave open

eye
positions

Button-Eyed Croc

6 mm (¼ in)

Eyes x 4
(two reversed)

Body x 2
(one reversed)
6 mm (¼ in) seam all round

leg positions

leg positions

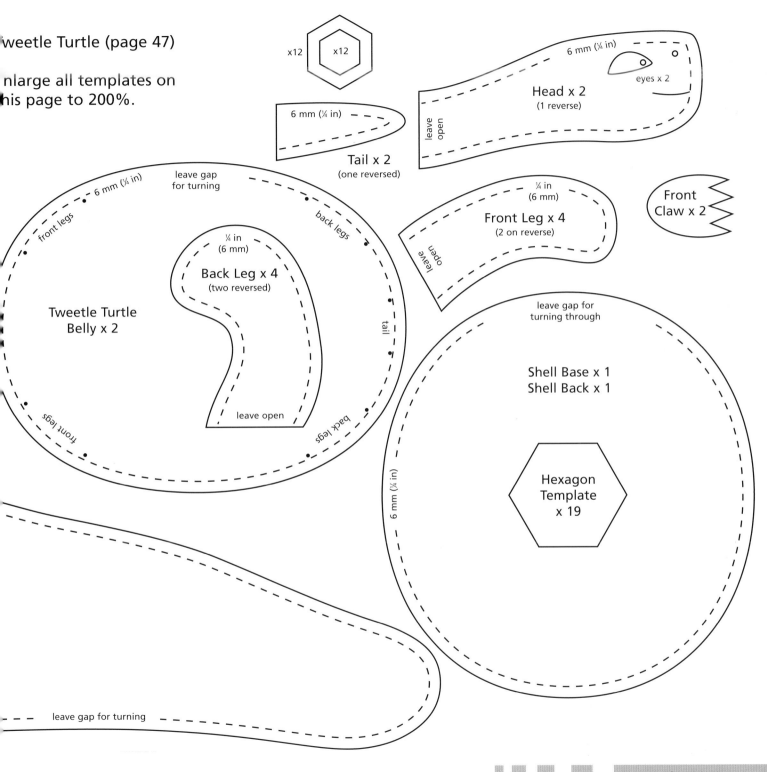

weetle Turtle (page 47)

nlarge all templates on
his page to 200%.

x12   x12

6 mm (¼ in)

Head x 2
(1 reverse)

eyes x 2

6 mm (¼ in)

Tail x 2
(one reversed)

leave open

leave gap
for turning

6 mm (¼ in)

front legs

back legs

¼ in
(6 mm)

Front Leg x 4
(2 on reverse)

leave open

Front
Claw x 2

Back Leg x 4
(two reversed)

¼ in
(6 mm)

Tweetle Turtle
Belly x 2

tail

leave open

leave gap for
turning through

back legs

front legs

6 mm (¼ in)

Shell Base x 1
Shell Back x 1

Hexagon
Template
x 19

leave gap for turning

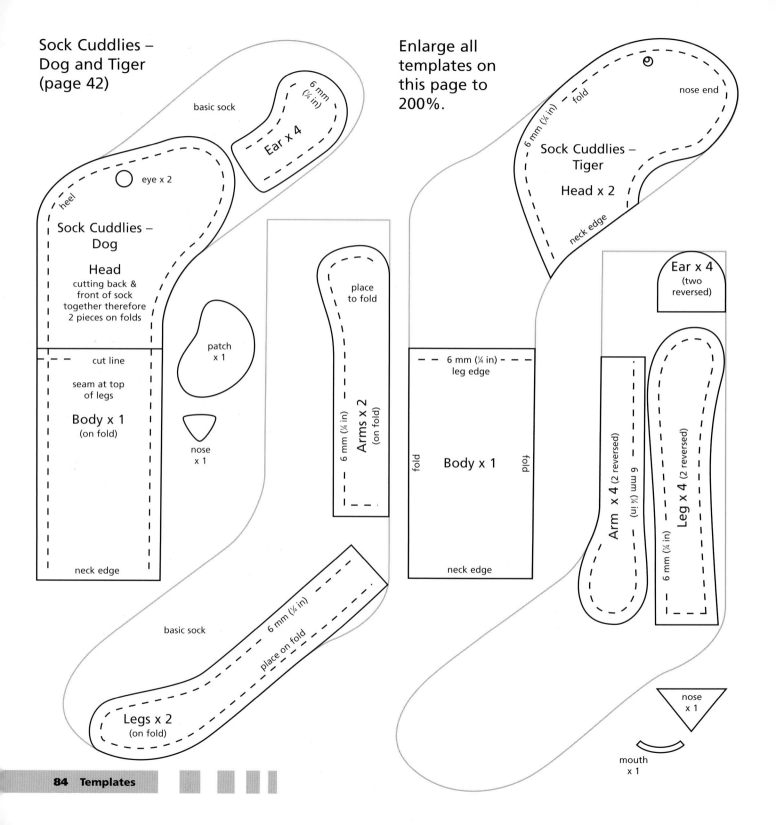

Sock Cuddlies –
Dog and Tiger
(page 42)

Enlarge all
templates on
this page to
200%.

basic sock

6 mm
(¼ in)

Ear x 4

eye x 2

heel

Sock Cuddlies –
Dog

Head

cutting back &
front of sock
together therefore
2 pieces on folds

cut line

seam at top
of legs

Body x 1
(on fold)

neck edge

patch
x 1

nose
x 1

place
to fold

6 mm (¼ in)

Arms x 2
(on fold)

basic sock

6 mm (¼ in)

place on fold

Legs x 2
(on fold)

6 mm (¼ in)   fold

nose end

Sock Cuddlies –
Tiger

Head x 2

neck edge

Ear x 4
(two
reversed)

6 mm (¼ in)
leg edge

fold

Body x 1

fold

neck edge

Arm x 4 (2 reversed)

6 mm (¼ in)

Leg x 4 (2 reversed)

6 mm (¼ in)

nose
x 1

mouth
x 1

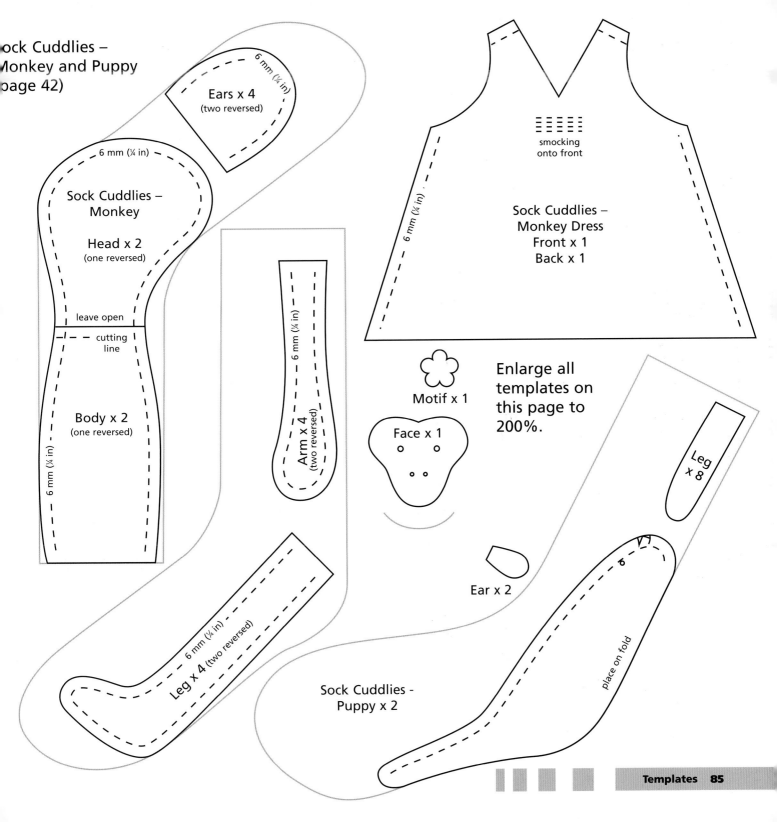

Sock Cuddlies –
Monkey and Puppy
(page 42)

Ears x 4
(two reversed)

6 mm (¼ in)

6 mm (¼ in)

Sock Cuddlies –
Monkey

Head x 2
(one reversed)

leave open

cutting line

Body x 2
(one reversed)

6 mm (¼ in)

6 mm (¼ in)

Arm x 4
(two reversed)

smocking onto front

6 mm (¼ in)

Sock Cuddlies –
Monkey Dress
Front x 1
Back x 1

Motif x 1

Face x 1

Enlarge all
templates on
this page to
200%.

Leg
x 8

Ear x 2

6 mm (¼ in)

Leg x 4 (two reversed)

place on fold

Sock Cuddlies -
Puppy x 2

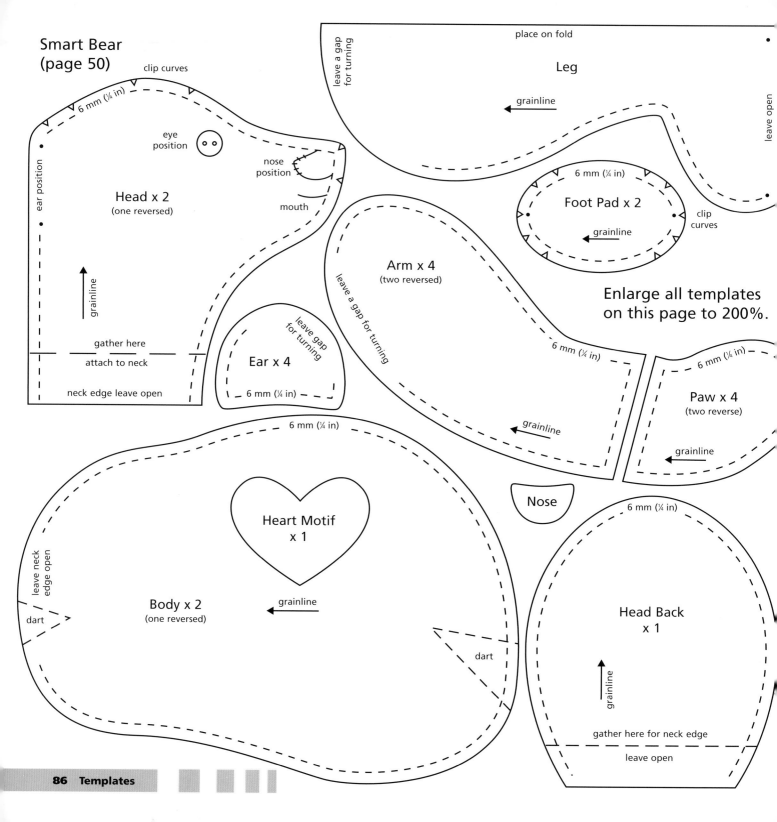

Smart Bear
(page 50)

clip curves

6 mm (¼ in)

eye position

nose position

mouth

ear position

Head x 2
(one reversed)

grainline

gather here

attach to neck

neck edge leave open

place on fold

Leg

leave a gap for turning

grainline

leave open

6 mm (¼ in)

Foot Pad x 2

grainline

clip curves

Enlarge all templates
on this page to 200%.

Arm x 4
(two reversed)

leave a gap for turning

leave gap for turning

Ear x 4

6 mm (¼ in)

6 mm (¼ in)

grainline

6 mm (¼ in)

Paw x 4
(two reverse)

grainline

Nose

6 mm (¼ in)

Heart Motif
x 1

grainline

Body x 2
(one reversed)

leave neck edge open

dart

dart

Head Back
x 1

6 mm (¼ in)

grainline

gather here for neck edge

leave open

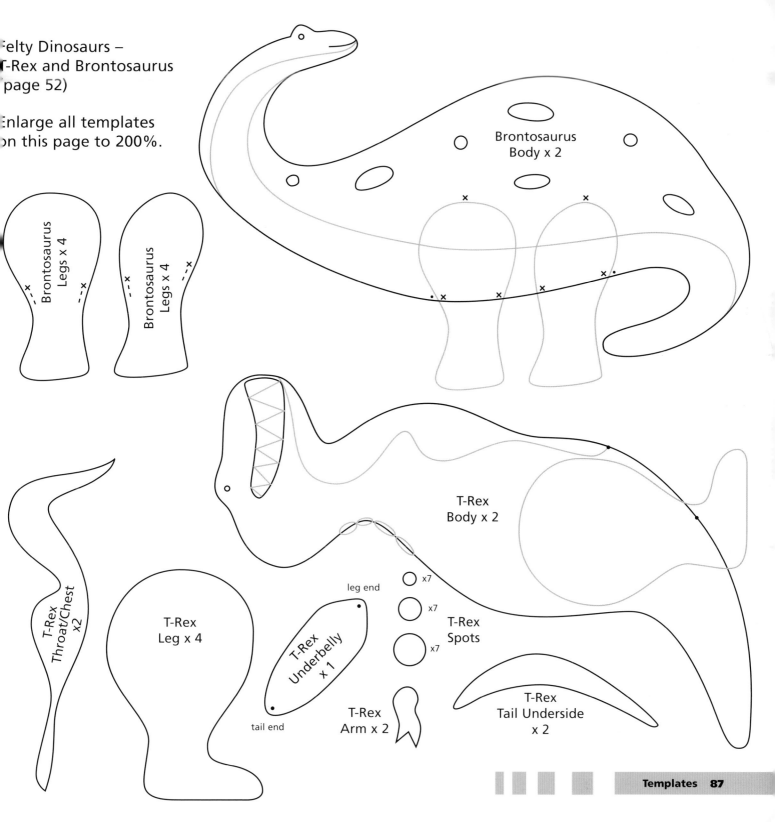

Felty Dinosaurs –
T-Rex and Brontosaurus
(page 52)

Enlarge all templates
on this page to 200%.

Brontosaurus
Legs x 4

Brontosaurus
Legs x 4

Brontosaurus
Body x 2

T-Rex
Body x 2

T-Rex
Throat/Chest
x2

T-Rex
Leg x 4

T-Rex
Underbelly
x 1

leg end

tail end

T-Rex
Arm x 2

x7

x7

x7

T-Rex
Spots

T-Rex
Tail Underside
x 2

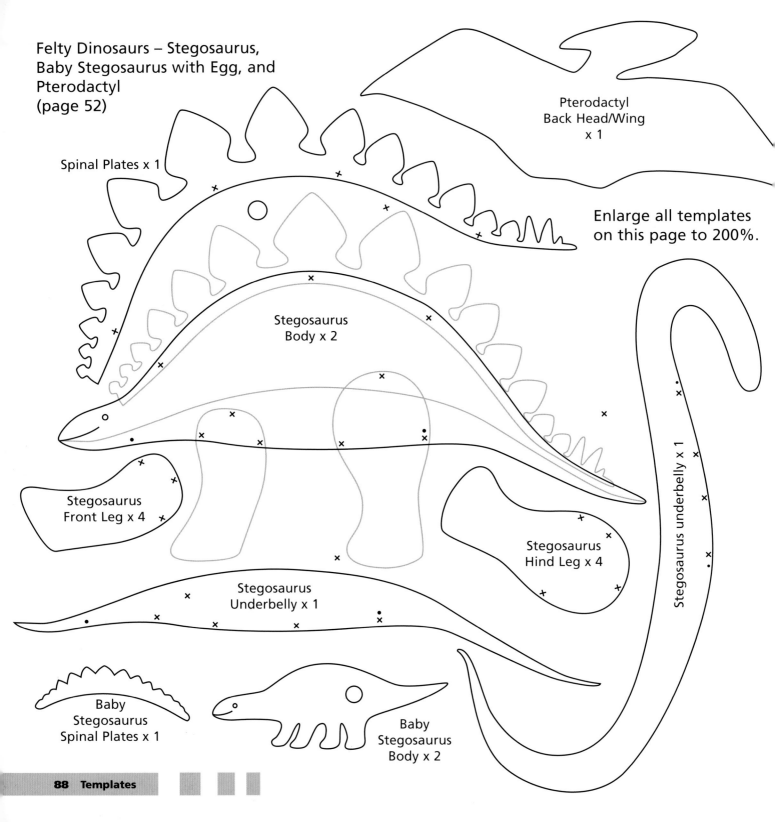

Felty Dinosaurs – Stegosaurus, Baby Stegosaurus with Egg, and Pterodactyl
(page 52)

Pterodactyl
Back Head/Wing
x 1

Spinal Plates x 1

Enlarge all templates
on this page to 200%.

Stegosaurus
Body x 2

Stegosaurus underbelly x 1

Stegosaurus
Front Leg x 4

Stegosaurus
Hind Leg x 4

Stegosaurus
Underbelly x 1

Baby
Stegosaurus
Spinal Plates x 1

Baby
Stegosaurus
Body x 2

Felty Dinosaurs –
Dino Toy Egg Bag and
Pterodactyl
(page 52)

Pterodactyl
Inside Wing x 1

Pterodactyl
Body x 1

Enlarge all templates
on this page to 200%.

6 mm (¼ in)

Egg Bag
x 2

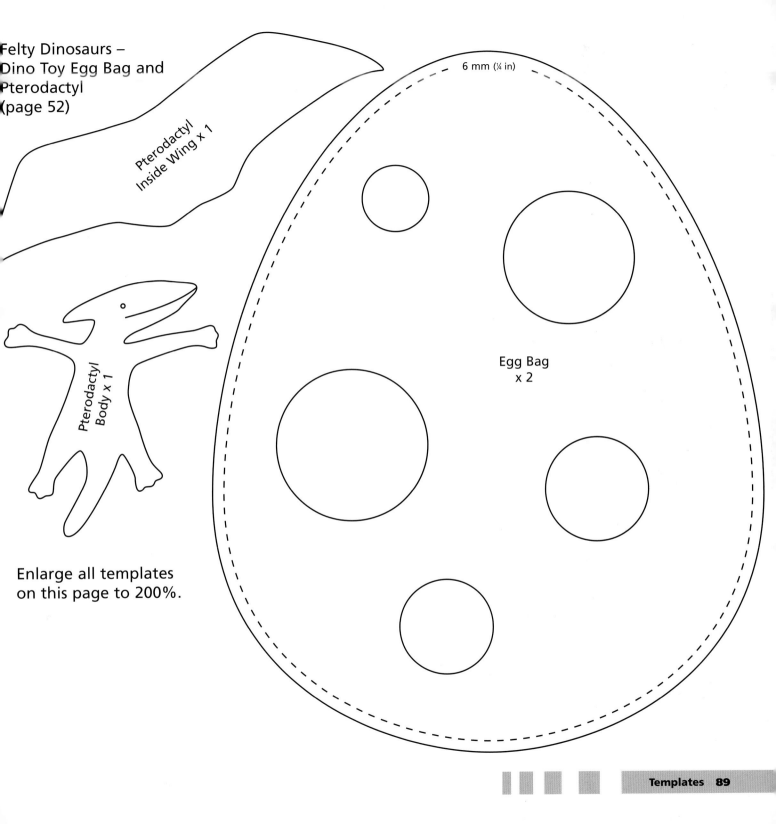

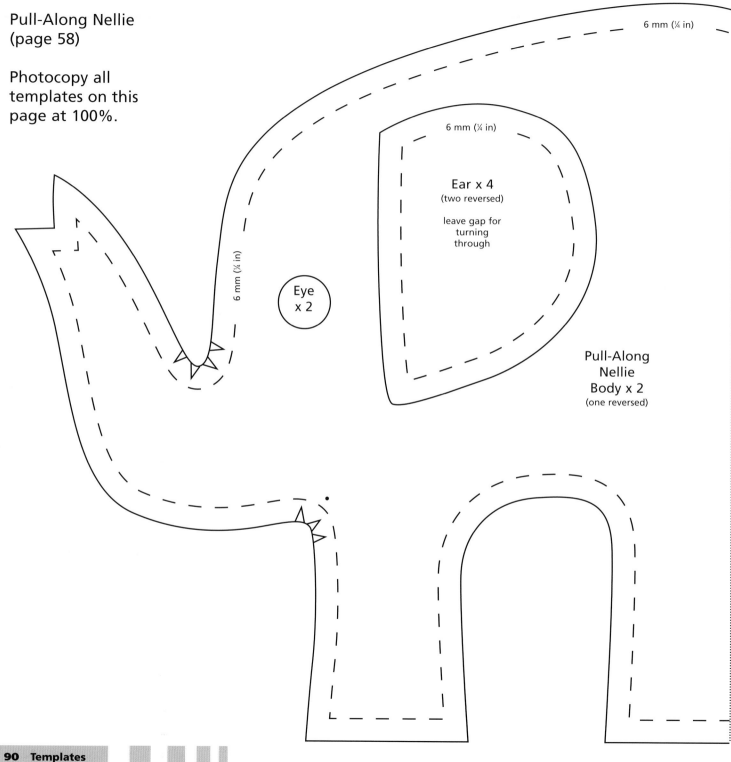

Pull-Along Nellie
(page 58)

Photocopy all
templates on this
page at 100%.

6 mm (¼ in)

6 mm (¼ in)

Ear x 4
(two reversed)

leave gap for
turning
through

6 mm (¼ in)

Eye
x 2

Pull-Along
Nellie
Body x 2
(one reversed)

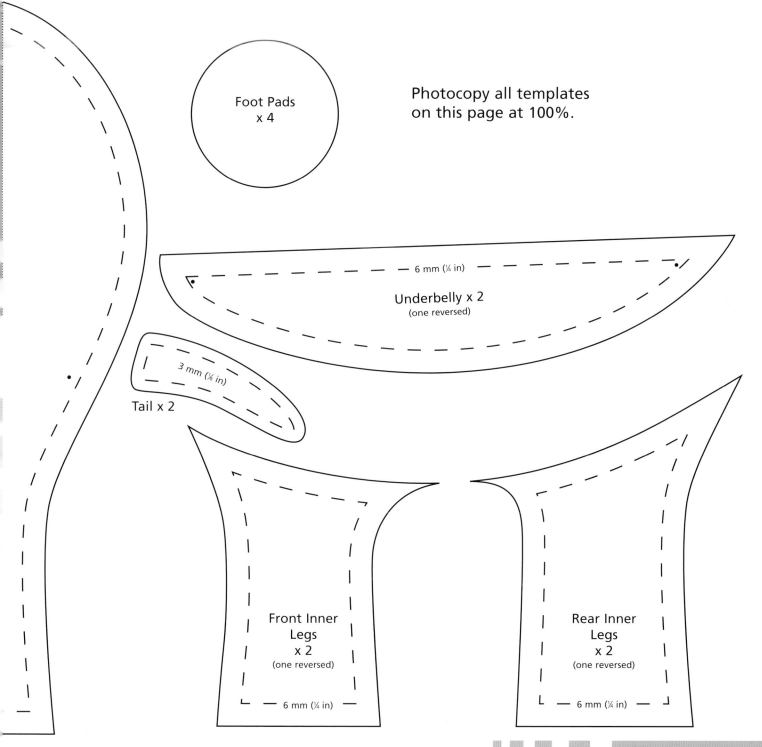

Foot Pads
x 4

Photocopy all templates
on this page at 100%.

— 6 mm (¼ in) —

Underbelly x 2
(one reversed)

3 mm (⅛ in)

Tail x 2

Front Inner
Legs
x 2
(one reversed)

— 6 mm (¼ in) —

Rear Inner
Legs
x 2
(one reversed)

— 6 mm (¼ in) —

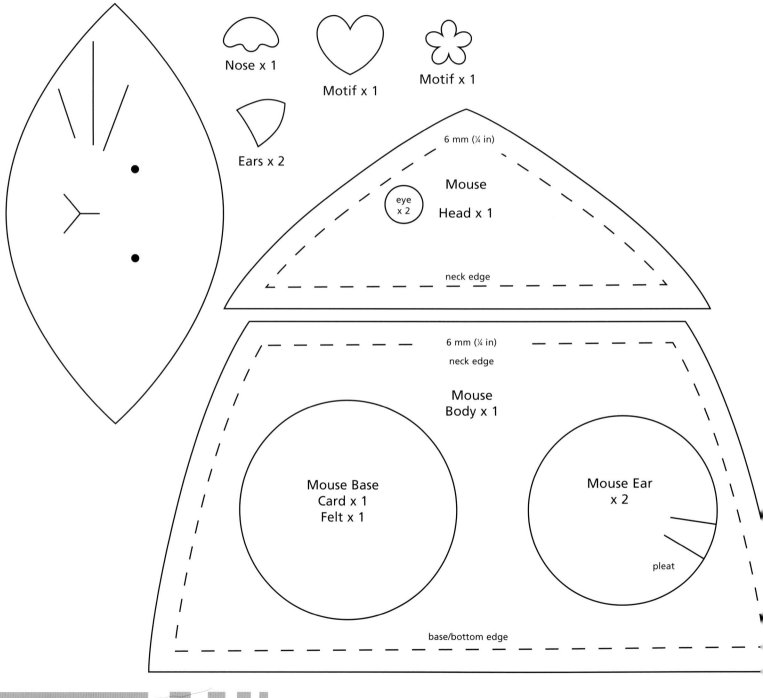

Nose x 1

Motif x 1

Motif x 1

Ears x 2

6 mm (¼ in)

Mouse

eye
x 2

Head x 1

neck edge

6 mm (¼ in)

neck edge

Mouse
Body x 1

Mouse Base
Card x 1
Felt x 1

Mouse Ear
x 2

pleat

base/bottom edge

Hobby Horse
(page 60)

Enlarge all templates on
this page to 200%.

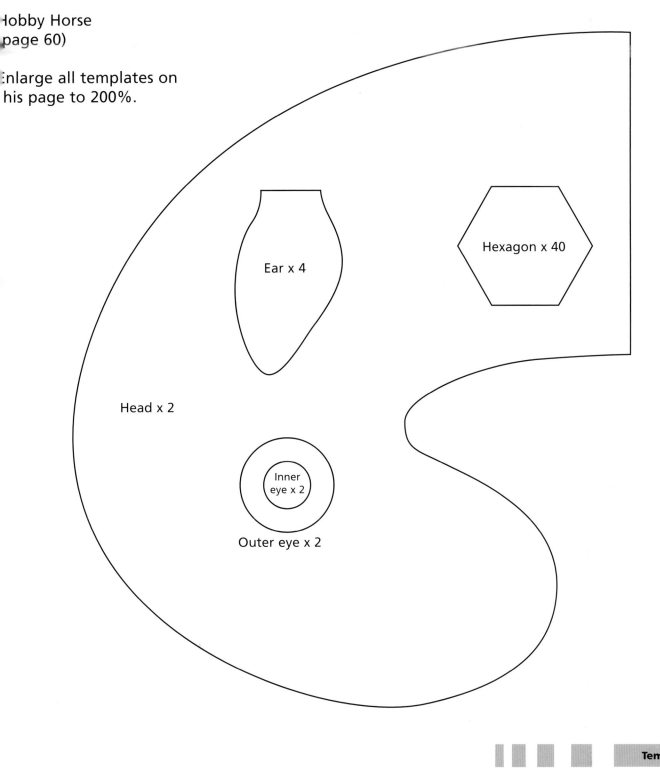

Ear x 4

Hexagon x 40

Head x 2

Inner
eye x 2

Outer eye x 2

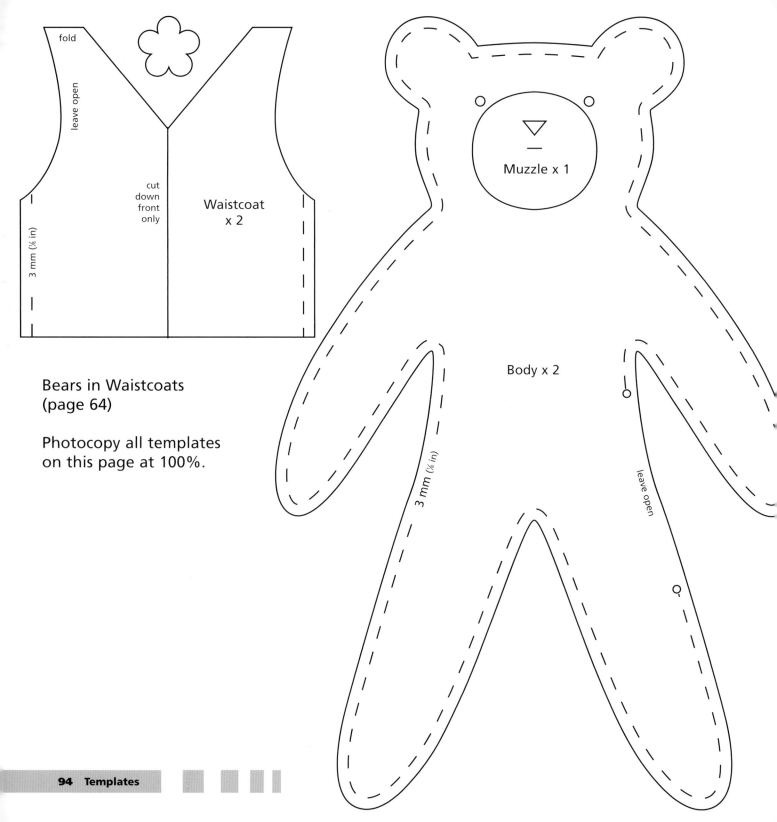

fold

leave open

3 mm (⅛ in)

cut down front only

Waistcoat x 2

Bears in Waistcoats
(page 64)

Photocopy all templates
on this page at 100%.

Muzzle x 1

Body x 2

3 mm (⅛ in)

leave open

Coffee Pot Lid x 1

Retro Tea Set
(page 66)

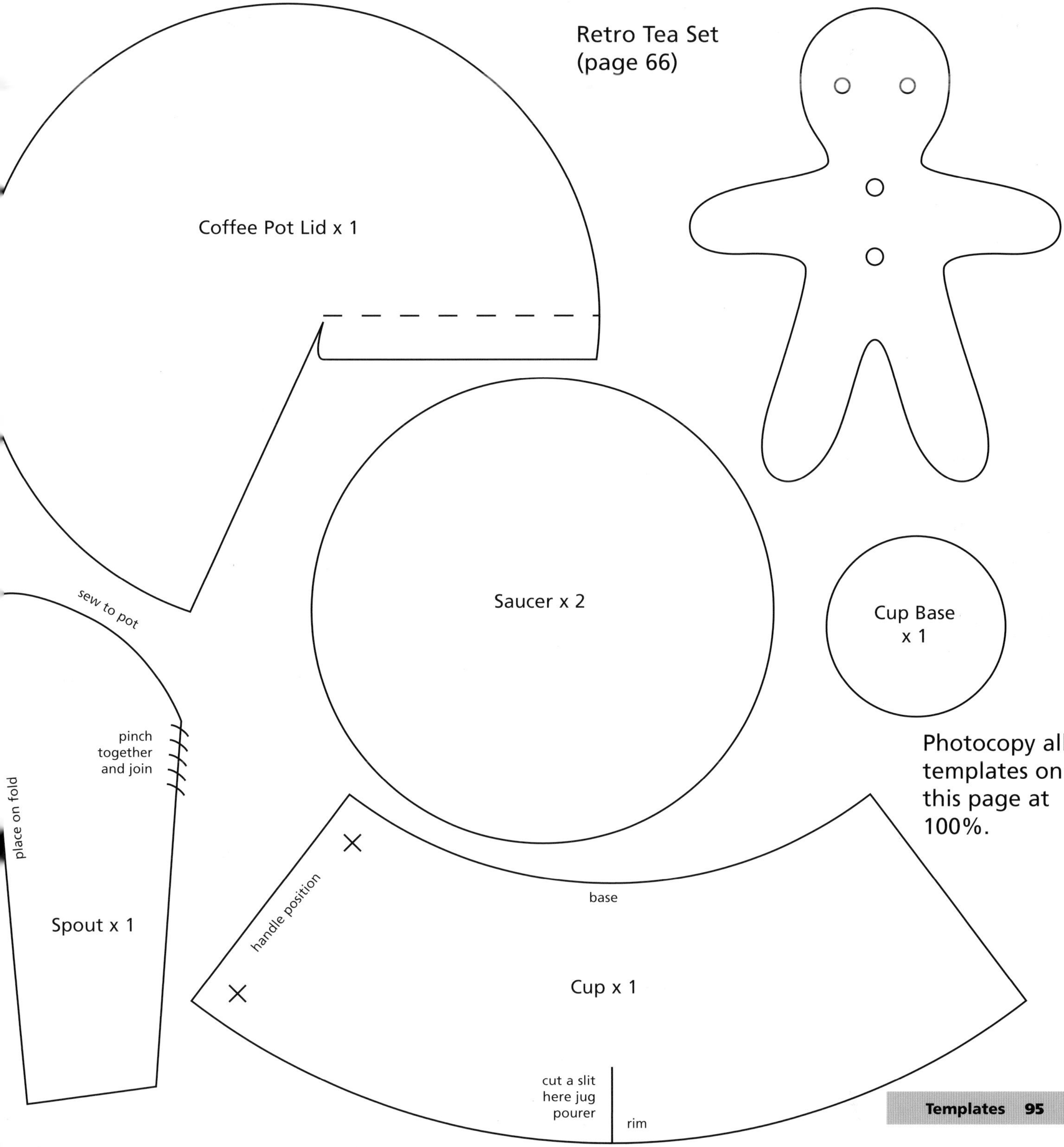

sew to pot

pinch
together
and join

place on fold

Spout x 1

Saucer x 2

Cup Base
x 1

Photocopy all
templates on
this page at
100%.

handle position

base

Cup x 1

cut a slit
here jug
pourer

rim

Acknowledgements

First off, I'd like to thank Marie Clayton for inviting me to do this book – I hope you like it, Marie.

Thanks must also go to Katie Cowan and Michelle Lo for their friendly and helpful advice, also to Fiona Corbridge for her patient pattern checking – you're a star! I'd like to extend my gratitude to Mark Winwood for his magical photography and for making the toys 'come alive'.

And finally, to my three long-suffering children, who see me making the toys and then watch yearningly as they are taken away and sent off to London. A big sorry – Harry, May and James! I'll make you all something soon.